DATE DUE			

A HISTORY OF HARMONIC THEORY IN THE UNITED STATES

A History of

HARMONIC THEORY

in the United States

DAVID M. THOMPSON

The Kent State University Press

Grateful acknowledgment is made to the following publishers for permission to quote and to use musical examples from the following sources: from Allen I. McHose, *Basic Principles of the Technique of 18th and 19th Century Composition*, ©Allen Irvine McHose, reprinted by permission of the author; from Percy Goetschius, *The Structure of Music*, © 1934, Theodore Presser Company, used by permission of the publisher; from Donald Tweedy, *Manual of Harmonic Technic*, ©1928 Oliver Ditson Company, used by permission of Theodore Presser Company; from Heinrich Schenker, *Harmony*, Oswald Jones, ed., translated by Elizabeth Mann Borghese, 1954, reprinted by permission of The University of Chicago Press; from Roger Sessions, *Harmonic Practice*, copyright 1951 by Harcourt Brace Jovanovich, Inc., renewed 1979 by Roger Sessions and reprinted by permission of the publisher; from Allen Forte, *Tonal Harmony in Concept and Practice*, copyright ©1962 by Holt, Rinehart and Winston, Inc., and reprinted by permission of the publisher; from Walter Piston, *Harmony*, Third Edition, with the permission of W. W. Norton & Company, Inc., copyright 1941, 1948, ©1962 by W. W. Norton & Company, Inc., copyright renewed 1969 by Walter Piston; from William Mitchell, *Elementary Harmony* and Allen I. McHose, *The Contrapuntal Harmonic Technique of the 18th Century*, used by permission of Prentice-Hall, Inc.; from George Wedge, *Applied Harmony*, 2 vol., 1930-31, with the permission of G. Schirmer, Inc.; from Carleton Bullis, *Harmonic Forms*, 1933, with the permission of Carl F. Ludwig Music Publishing Company.

Library of Congress Cataloging in Publication Data

Thompson, David M

    A history of harmonic theory in the United States.

    Bibliography: p.
    Includes index.
    1. Harmony—History. 2. Music—Theory—History.
I. Title.
ML444.T5   781.3′0973   80-82202
ISBN 0-87338-246-3

Contents

McHose
The Influence of Heinrich Schenker: William
Mitchell, Allen Forte

Preface

This work traces the lines of development of the most important concepts in the theory of harmony in the writings of American theorists. Beginning with American editions of nineteenth-century European works on harmony, it follows the development of harmonic thought through the work of Percy Goetschius and his contemporaries and students to the writings of Walter Piston, Allen McHose, and Allen Forte.

It should be emphasized that this work is not intended as a history of theorists, but of ideas. Biographical information is sometimes included, but is kept at a minimum so that attention may be devoted to the development of theoretical concepts. Also, theories of twentieth-century harmony have been excluded, as have theories of jazz harmony. The development of these theories is presently at too early a stage to justify regarding them as history.

There has been an interest in the history of music theory ever since the appearance of Hugo Riemann's *Geschichte der Musik-theorie im IX.-XIX. Jahrhundert* in 1898. The interest in the subject is evident at the present time in the United States, as various schools and university departments of music offer courses in the history of theory. Interest in the subject is certainly laudable, for students who are preparing to become teachers of theory ought to know something of the history of their profession. However, Riemann's *Geschichte* does not relate theoretical developments later than the middle of the nineteenth century. The other vehicle, Matthew Shirlaw's *Theory of Harmony*, stops at 1901 with the Victorian English theorists. Thus there is a gap between the periods covered by these works and the material which the modern American theory teacher finds himself teaching in class. I hope that the present work will help to fill that gap.

It would be impossible for anyone to undertake a project such as this one without the assistance of a number of people. I wish to express my gratitude to my wife, Patricia, for her valuable assistance with this project, especially for undertaking the typing of the original manuscript. Also, I am grateful to Dr. James Waters, Dr. Walter Watson, Mr. Hugh Glauser, and Dr. Terry Kuhn, my colleagues at the Kent State University School of Music, for their encouragement and for their numerous helpful comments and suggestions.

1
Antecedents

European Theories of Harmony in the United States in the Nineteenth Century

In 1846 a German book on music, translated into English, appeared in print in the United States. The translator's Preface began thus:

> The origin of the enterprise which the translator has undertaken, in rendering into English the present work, is traceable to a fact in his own experience. When, some years since, he commenced a more methodical and thorough course of musical studies, he at once found himself without the requisite helps. Notwithstanding he possessed himself of such books as could be found in this country, there still remained a most obvious and important deficiency. These books were all perceived to be defective in two particulars; first, in *the absolute want of matter*, and secondly, in *the manner of communication*. A great many things which were continually sought for, and which it is seriously important to every musical student to know, were not to be met with in any of them. Thus a deficiency was seen to exist, which must leave the mind in ignorance, conjecture, and doubt, on many points most vitally concerned with musical knowledge and musical practice. Indeed, this defectiveness extends even to matters involved in common, every-day musical performance; and so great is the chasm which it leaves in all the instructions relating to Harmony and Composition, that the latter can scarcely be said to be taught at all.[1]

The translator was the American writer James F. Warner, of Boston. The work under translation was Gottfried Weber's treatise *Versuch einer geordneten Theorie der Tonsetzkunst* (*Theory of Musical Composition*).

Warner was justified in his complaint about the lack of works on music theory available in the United States, for in 1846 music was considered by most Americans to be either a church activity or a recreational pastime and was rarely regarded as a fit subject for serious study. Only four years had passed since Lowell Mason had managed to persuade the Boston School Committee to become the first American school system to admit music to its curriculum. The openings of music academies and conservatories of music in Boston and New York were at least a decade in the future. Moreover, the pedagogical books on music available in the United States dealt with practical considerations rather than theoretical ones. Typical were the singing-school books with their shaped-note systems, which had been in print since 1803. It is no wonder, then, that Warner turned to the German writers for information on harmonic theory.

Warner recognized that most of the German treatises on harmony were too speculative for American tastes. The American reader, who was most likely unacquainted with even the rudiments of harmony, would certainly become impatient with extensive demonstrations of the harmonic series or lists of rules for discovering chords amid huge stacks of thirds. Warner selected the *Theorie der Tonsetzkunst* because he felt that Weber's unique practical approach to harmonic theory, which had made his treatise popular in Europe, would be ideally suited to American readers. "Weber's work is pre-eminently adapted to *this country*. Its admirably clear and simple style, taken in connection with the copious detail of its matter, renders it, as the author himself very justly observes, peculiarly appropriate to those who have but little or no present acquaintance with the subject. It is truly just the book that we need."[2]

Following the appearance of Weber's treatise on harmony, translations of several other German works were published in the United States. In 1851 the *Theory and Practice of Musical Composition*, a translation by Hermann S. Saroni of Adolph Bernard Marx's *Kompositionslehre*, was published in New York by F. J. Huntington, and Mason and Law. The appealing features of the work, according to a review in *Dwight's Journal of Music*, were "the unity, the naturalness, the clearness, the completeness, and the charm" with which Marx presented his subject. The reviewer went on to pronounce Marx's approach superior to Weber's: "Marx is a believer in musical Science, in the possibility of referring all the elements of the art back to a unitary central principle, and not a mere empiric like Godfrey Weber."[3] It would seem, then, that at least a few American musicians were interested in a more "scientific" treatment of music theory than Weber's pragmatic approach gave them.

With the appearance in the 1860s of the first American music conservatories, a demand arose for a harmony textbook that had neither the great length of Weber's treatise (Warner's translation required two volumes totaling 826 pages) nor the speculative aspect of Marx's work. This need was answered by the publication of the *Manual of Harmony* (New York: G. Schirmer, 1867), a translation of the *Lehrbuch der Harmonie* of Ernst Freidrich Richter, professor at the Leipzig Conservatory. Richter was a follower of Gottfried Weber, and like Weber he believed in a practical approach to harmony. It was probably this element, as well as the brevity of the book, that made it popular in the newly formed conservatories and music departments of American colleges. Richter's *Manual* was used at the Conservatory of Music at Oberlin College. John Knowles Paine used it in his harmony class at Harvard University.[4] Its popularity even extended into the twentieth century; its last American printing, by G. Schirmer, was in 1912.

Richter's influence in America extended beyond his *Lehrbuch der Harmonie.* Several important musicians in America had actually studied harmony with Richter in Leipzig. John P. Morgan, who made the first American translation of the *Lehrbuch,* was a former Richter student, as were Theodore Baker, of the staff of G. Schirmer, and Stephen Emery and James C. D. Parker, both professors at the New England Conservatory.

Moreover, a few Americans were writing theory texts themselves. James C. D. Parker's *Manual of Harmony and Thorough Bass* (Boston: Nathan Richardson, 1855) was among the first of these. It was a short work (190 pages) and largely echoed Richter. However, it contained a few deviations from Richter's theory, and the review of the work in *Dwight's Journal* took exception to one of them:

> he adopts the usual confused and unscientific definition of the Minor
> Scale, a definition derived from the Signature rather than the thing

signified. "As this Minor Scale contains the same tones with the major scale, it must have the same signature." But the minor scale does *not* contain the same tones as its relative major. The scale of A minor has not the same tones with that of C major; it differs in that its G must be sharp. This the harmony requires; and the only true scale is that furnished by the harmony, i.e., the chords of the tonic, dominant, and subdominant.[5]

The reviewer's firm belief in the tonic, dominant, and subdominant triads as the origin of the scale, a basic concept in the Weber-Richter theory, is an interesting indication of the inroads that this theory had already made in the United States.

It was only in the last quarter of the nineteenth century that American musicians became interested in the speculative theory of harmony. This was supplied to them, not by German writers, but by the theorists of Victorian England. The first British work on harmony to appear in the United States was Sir John Stainer's *Harmony, with an Appendix Containing One Hundred Graduated Exercises*, which was issued by Novello, Ewer and Company in New York in 1877. It was only a short textbook, however, and contained very little of Stainer's unique theory of harmony.[6] Later British works on harmony to appear in the United States were actually treatises on the speculative theory that had developed in England, such as Ebenezer Prout's *Harmony, its Theory and Practice*, which was issued by G. Schirmer in New York in 1889 (the same year it was first published in London), and George A. Macfarren's *Six Lectures on Harmony*, issued from New York in 1892. The influence of the British theorists, however, would be felt as much through the harmonic theory of Percy Goetschius as through the appearance of their own works in America.

The German Theorists: Gottfried Weber, Ernst Friedrich Richter, Immanuel Faisst

By the time Gottfried Weber's *Versuch einer geordneten Theorie der Tonsetzkunst* appeared in the United States in 1842, it had already achieved popularity in Europe. The reason for its wide acceptance among European musicians was its practical, uncomplicated approach to theory, the same feature that made it appropriate for American publication.

Weber's *Theorie der Tonsetzkunst*, written in 1817–21, was welcomed as a relief from the other writings on harmony and composition that were circulating in Europe at the beginning of the nineteenth century. There were essentially three schools of harmonic theory in the early 1800s. The oldest of these was the figured-bass system, a survival from Baroque practice. Its long lists of rules were based entirely on the intervals of notes above the bass. Another group of theorists, seeking to classify chords, took as a basis Rameau's concept of "chords by supposition" and developed huge "fundamental" harmonies by stacking thirds atop one another. A third group of theorists took the acoustical theory of Zarlino and Rameau as a starting point and tried to manipulate the harmonic series and derive from it the major and minor scales as well as the most common chords in musical use at the time. As these three schools developed alongside each other, criticizing each other and borrowing ideas from each other, they presented the European musician with an increasingly complicated and bewildering picture of harmonic theory. It was just this confusion that Weber sought to eliminate in his *Theorie der Tonsetzkunst*.

Weber's idea of the purpose of harmonic theory is shown in his criticism of the figured-bass approach to harmony. His objection to the litanies of rules, typical of the figured-bass treatises of the time, is that despite their copiousness these rules do not describe the qualities of the chords but are merely sets of directions. In one of his "Remarks" he asks,

How much rationality is exhibited in the fact, that all our books of instruction on musical composition hitherto have, from beginning to end, devoted themselves to the business of showing how a tone which stands at a distance of such and such a number of degrees from the bass tone, as e.g. the third or fourth of the bass tone, etc. may be treated, prepared, resolved—regarded as a so-called consonance or dissonance—and how it is to be doubled or not doubled, and the like, and the fact that all our theoretical writers hitherto have made the entire doctrine of musical composition depend solely and exclusively upon consideration of the distance of this or that tone from the bass tone, and instead of attending to the essential and fundamental *properties* of the different harmonic combinations and of each of their elements, they give us rather a troublesome set of mere casuistic prescriptions upon the treatment of the intervals of the bass tone.[7]

Weber's objection is certainly a valid one. Figured-bass symbols, taken alone, might indicate a few qualities of a chord, such as the relative stability of a $\frac{5}{3}$ chord in comparison with a $\frac{6}{3}$ chord, or the presence of dissonance in a seventh-chord. Nonetheless, the information provided by these symbols is inadequate as a foundation for a theory of harmony. The figured-bass system does not explicitly state the relationship between the inversions of a chord—for instance, that the $\frac{5}{3}$ chord on the first degree of the scale contains the same members as the $\frac{6}{3}$ chord on the third scale degree. Moreover, the same figured-bass symbol may represent chords requiring different treatment, depending on the scale degree of the bass tone. A seventh-chord on the tonic is treated differently than a dominant seventh-chord. The cause of these inadequacies is quite simply the early origin of the figured-bass system. Its rules had been developed long before the time of Rameau, who was the first to describe such phenomena as harmonic inversion and the unique qualities of the dominant seventh-chord. The figured-bass system had never been revised to include these concepts.

Weber argues that the rules of the figured-bass theories result from inadequate observation of musical practice. He accuses the figured-bass theorists of observing only a few examples in musical practice and then using these to formulate rules which they attempt to apply universally.[8] Weber apparently does not realize that the underlying fault of the figured-bass system is that it is out of date not only theoretically but also musically. Figured-bass had been obsolete as an element of keyboard practice even before Mozart and Beethoven had begun to add new harmonic combinations to the musical vocabulary. Thus, the figured-bass theorists' observation of musical practice is understandably limited to the harmonic usage found in earlier Baroque music.[9]

Weber criticizes the theory of stacked thirds on the ground that it is needlessly complicated. The idea of constructing a number of "fundamental" ninth-, eleventh-, and thirteenth-chords by stacking thirds atop one another apparently originated with Georg Andreas Sorge[10] and was developed in the works of Abt Vogler and more especially in the works of his student Justin Heinrich Knecht. With the appearance of Knecht's *Elementarwerk der Harmonie* in 1792, the system reached a disgraceful degree of complication. Weber, in one of his caustic "Remarks," derides Knecht's theory of 3,600 different chords, among which 720 are "fundamental" chords with such elegant names as "the great-small-great agreeable thirteenth-eleventh-ninth-seventh-chords," or "the small-diminished-small sad-sounding thirteenth-eleventh-ninth-seventh-chords." Weber remarks that "the whole catalogue would fill more than fifteen pages quarto."[11]

Weber's opinion is that neither nature nor musical practice determines any single "correct" system of classification of chords. Chord classifications are arbitrary delineations made by theorists: "Men dispute and contend and quarrel on the question, how many fundamental harmonies there are—a contention which, as it occurs to me, is about as illimitable as that on the question, how many *genera* of plants there are in nature, when nature herself certainly knows nothing of all the *genera* which have been invented by human ingenuity."[12] The theorist's duty, then, is not to search for some correct set of basic chord formations, but rather to invent the most convenient system possible, that is, "to bring the greatest possible number of species agreeing with one another in the largest number of characteristics under the smallest possible number of principal classes."[13] As will be seen, Weber's own system of classification recognizes only seven basic chord types, a markedly more convenient arrangement than Knecht's 720 "fundamental" chords.

The main thrust of Weber's objections to the acoustical theories of harmony is aimed at the question of the appropriateness of their appearance in treatises dealing with harmonic practice. Weber recognizes that there are natural laws that govern musical sound (or any sound, for that matter). He even acknowledges the study of musical acoustics as an established branch of theory.[14] However, he is opposed to the custom of using it as the basis for a practical study of harmony:

> Most teachers of musical composition imagine that the theory of musical composition must necessarily be founded on harmonic acoustics, and on this account, commence their books of instruction with arithmetical and algebraic problems and formulas . . . it is, in my honest conviction, a mistake of teachers of musical composition,

betraying a decided want of understanding of the subject, to mix, as they do, with the doctrine of musical composition, such demonstrations by fractions, powers, roots, and equations, and other mathematical formulas, from which *to proceed* in teaching the theory of musical composition.[15]

Weber does take the opportunity to spar with the current acoustical theories. He contends that the inaudibility of the harmonics of a tone prevents these harmonics from affecting music at all. If even the first five harmonics were audible, he says, then upon the sounding of the chord at *a* in Figure 1, the several harmonic series shown at *b* would be produced, and the audible result would be the hideous combination shown at *c*.

Figure 1.   Weber, p. 16

Weber thus declares that "the associated sounding of the accessory tones of a string is so far from belonging to the essential nature or to the beauty of a musical sound, that the positive injuriousness of such an imperfection is prevented only by the inaudibleness of these associated tones."[16]

Weber points out the folly of attempting to derive the major scale from the harmonic series. He correctly observes that if the C major scale were to be formed from the natural harmonics of C, then not only E and G would be produced but also a B-flat, which is foreign to the key and too flat anyway. Such a scale would also contain an F that is a quarter-tone too sharp and an A that is too high.[17]

Weber discusses the acoustical explanation of the minor triad which was proposed by Rameau and Tartini. According to this explanation, the fifth of the minor triad is not only the third (and sixth) harmonic of the root but also the fifth harmonic of the minor third. In the minor triad shown in Figure 2, G is a harmonic both of C and of E-flat. The minor harmony is then the opposite of the major; whereas the major triad is made up of a fundamental and two of its harmonics, the minor triad consists of a harmonic and two of its possible fundamentals. Although Weber presents this theory in a scornful tone, he offers no specific objections to it.[18] Rather, he appends it to Rameau's derivation of the major and minor scales from the notes of the tonic, subdominant, and dominant triads[19]; and then criticizes Rameau for presenting a theory which is based partly on acoustics and partly on arbitrary explanation.[20] Weber actually uses the word "arbitrary" to describe this explanation of the origin of the scale; apparently he does not object to arbitrariness, since in another chapter he uses exactly the same explanation of the scale as did Rameau.

Figure 2. Derivation of the minor triad

In contrast to his predecessors, Weber does not base his harmonic theory on acoustics or long list of rules, and he uses only the leanest possible system of classification of chords. Rather than using the harmonic series as a source from which to derive harmony, he observes the harmonic combinations in the music of his time and summarizes them. Rather than giving strict rules, he makes general observations. "All that the theory of musical composition can do, consists chiefly in searching out those progressions which are usually found to be repugnant and disagreeable to our ear, in deducing therefrom rules which generally (hardly universally!) hold good, and in warning, by means of these, against disagreeable progressions."[21] The result is a system that is at least applicable to harmonic practice, even if its logic is sometimes shaky.

Weber begins by listing seven fundamental chord types (see Figure 3). He presents three types of triads, namely, major, minor, and diminished, and four seventh-chords, namely, dominant, major, minor, and half-diminished. He designates the dominant seventh-chord the "principal" seventh-chord because he observes that it is the most frequently used of the chords of the seventh. The others are "secondary" seventh-chords. "Every harmonic combination admits of being regarded as springing from one of these seven fundamental harmonies, and of being referred to one of them and explained as a modification of it, however varied and complicated it may appear."[22]

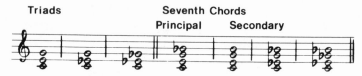

Figure 3.   *Fundamental chord types (Weber)*

The most unusual feature of Weber's fundamental chord system is the inclusion of the diminished triad and the half-diminished seventh-chord. Theorists had generally considered a chord to be dissonant if it contained a diminished fifth, and Weber recognizes this. This does not affect his system, however, because he uses triads to define consonance and dissonance, rather than the reverse: "The technical word *consonance* always affords us a convenient common name for the fundamental tone, its proper third and fifth, while the word *dissonance* gives us a name for every tone which is not the fundamental tone, nor its third, nor its fifth, but is something else."[23] By his definition, then, the diminished fifth is a consonant interval whenever it occurs between the fundamental and the fifth of a diminished triad.

According to Weber, the seven fundamental harmonies are capable of transformation not only by inversion and various types of spacing but also by chromatic alteration and by the addition of independent ninths. For instance, the third of the half-diminished seventh-chord may be chromatically raised, as shown in Figure 4 at *a*, producing a variation of the original fundamental chord. Also, the root of the chord might be omitted, as at *b*, and a ninth might be added, as at *c*. Each of these chords may then be inverted, so that they may assume the forms shown at *d*.[24] Thus Weber explains the chords that have come to be known as the French, Italian, and German augmented sixth-chords.

Figure 4.   Weber, p. 210

Weber devotes a great deal of attention to the transformation of harmony by the addition of independent ninths. An "independent" ninth is a tone a ninth above the fundamental and is considered neither an essential part of the chord nor a nonharmonic tone.[25] It is apparently a sort of half-member of the harmony, with a curious status somewhere between harmonic and nonharmonic. The major ninth is usually added to the dominant seventh-chord in a major key, forming the combination shown at *a* in Figure 5, and the minor ninth is added to the dominant seventh-chord in a minor key, as at *b*.

Figure 5.   Weber, p. 208

The important concept of "equivocalness" of chords arises after Weber's statement that chords with independent ninths sometimes appear without their roots. A dominant seventh-chord with a major ninth and omitted root appears exactly the same as the fundamental half-diminished seventh-chord, and confusion seems imminent. However, Weber vindicates himself by describing the chord an "equivocal" chord, or a chord with two possible meanings. He then distinguishes between the fundamental half-diminished seventh-chord and the dominant major-ninth-chord with the omitted root by referring to the context in which the chord appears. If it acts as a dominant chord by leading to a tonic, as in Figure 6 at *a*, then it should be considered a dominant ninth-chord. If it is being used as in *b*, where its function makes clear that the seventh scale degree is the real root, then it is a genuine fundamental half-diminished seventh-chord.[26] This and similar applications of the concept of harmonic "equivocalness" form one of the most distinctive features of Weber's entire system. Weber recognizes that a meaningful analysis of a chord depends on examination not only of the chord's construction but also of the harmonic context in which it appears. To analyze a chord a theorist must ask not only, "What notes are in it?" but also, "How is it behaving in the harmonic progression?" This is an important development in the recognition of the concept of harmonic function. It is probably the most positive result of Weber's use of practical observation as the basis of his harmonic theory.

Figure 6. Weber, p. 209

Weber's discussion of scales and tonality is less remarkable. He borrows from Rameau (without acknowledging him) the designation of the tonic, subdominant, and dominant triads as the three essential harmonies of a key. Since his theory has no acoustical foundation, he is forced to justify his selection of these three harmonies on the basis of his observation of musical practice, with such statements as, "We even find whole pieces of music, in which no other harmonies occur, than these most essential ones."[27] He has difficulty explaining the reason why the dominant triad in a minor key is always major even though the other two essential triads are minor; his best effort at explanation is, "Our spontaneous feeling, the organization of our musical ear, requires it to be so."[28]

Weber explains that the scale is formed by arranging the tones of the three essential harmonies of the key in a linear fashion. Since the subdominant triad is minor in a minor key, and the dominant is major, the only acceptable form of the minor scale is the harmonic form. This leads him to suggest that key signatures for minor keys be redesigned to accommodate the raised seventh scale degree, as shown in Figure 7.[29]

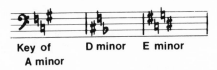

Key of   **D minor**   **E minor**
A minor

Figure 7. Weber, p. 281

On each tone of the major scale, Weber erects a fundamental triad and a fundamental seventh-chord whose spelling is consistent with that of the scale, as shown in Figure 8 at *a*. However, he finds that in the minor key he cannot place a fundamental seventh-chord on the seventh scale degree, since his fundamental seventh-chords do not include the fully diminished seventh. Moreover, he cannot spell any kind of harmony on the third degree because the augmented fifth is not present in any of his fundamental chords. His previous rejection of the lowered seventh in the minor scale prevents him from using a major triad on the third degree. He is thus forced to leave these positions conspicuously blank, as shown in Figure 8 (*b*).[30]

Figure 8. Weber, p. 234

Weber makes a distinction between nearly related and distantly related keys. His definition of nearly related keys depends on the constituency of the scales of the two keys under consideration. "Two keys whose scales have the highest degree of similarity to each other are called the most *nearly related keys.*"[31] The most nearly related keys to C major, then, include F and G major and A minor, whose scales each differ from that of C by one note only. However, Weber violates his own definition by including also the parallel minor key, C minor. He recognizes that its scale differs by two tones from that of C major. He says, however, that the common tonic of the two keys compensates for this, so that the two keys "have even too much in common with each other."[32]

Two keys which share a nearly related key are designated by Weber as having a "second grade of relationship."[33] The key of D major bears a second grade of relationship to C major, because both are nearly related keys to G major. The key of E-flat major is similarly related to C, since both have C minor as a near relative. Weber is then forced to admit that his "second grade of relationship" is inconsistent by his standard of similarity of scales; E-flat is really more distant from C than is D, since E-flat has one less note in common with C than does D.[34]

In discussing modulation, Weber sensibly takes into account the degree of permanence of the new key. If the modulation entirely eradicates the impression of the old tonality and convincingly replaces it with the new one, it is termed a "wholly digressive modulation." On the other hand, if after the modulation the feeling of the old key is still impressed upon the ear, the modulation is half-digressive.[35] Weber gives the example in Figure 9 as an illustration of half-digressive modulation. He points out that the dominant seventh-chord at the end of the first measure is such a temporary modulation that the feeling of C major as the tonic is still perfectly clear at the end of the example. He remarks that such modulations "are so very transient that they scarcely deserve the name,"[36] thus pointing out an uncertainty that would be resolved 120 years later by the discovery of the concept of the secondary dominant.

Throughout his treatise, Weber shows a predilection for inventing symbols. His proposed revision of the minor key

Figure 9. *Weber, p. 329*

signatures has already been mentioned. He devises a method of showing intervals by using arabic numerals and points. A figure with a point before it indicates a minor interval (•6), or a perfect fourth (•4), or diminished fifth (•5). A point after a numeral indicates that the interval is major (6•), or a perfect fifth (5•), or augmented fourth (4•).

Of greater significance is Weber's system of symbols for his fundamental chords. In this system, a capital letter represents a major triad (the letter shows the fundamental tone). A lowercase letter represents a minor triad. A lowercase letter preceded by a small circle ° indicates a diminished triad. The dominant seventh-chord is shown with an arabic numeral 7 after a capital letter; the minor seventh with a lowercase letter followed by a 7; the half-diminished seventh with a circle °, a lowercase letter, and a 7; and the major seventh with a capital letter and a 7 with a stroke through it.[37] Figure 10 shows the application of these symbols. Not shown in Figure 10 but also used in Weber's system: the presence of an independent ninth in a chord may be shown by an Arabic numeral 9. An Arabic 0 indicates a chord with an omitted root.

| C | c | °c | C7 | c7 | °c7 | C7̸ |

Figure 10. *Symbols for fundamental chord-types (Weber)*

In order to represent chords with respect to their positions in a key, Weber presents the system of Roman-numeral symbols that has since become familiar to every student of theory. Like the letter-name symbols for chords, the Roman numerals may be uppercase or lowercase or preceded by a circle °

to show whether the triads are major, minor, or diminished. Arabic numerals are again used to show sevenths, ninths, and omitted roots. The key in which the chords occupy their positions is shown by its letter-name followed by a colon, placed in front of the numerals as an index.[38] The use of these symbols is illustrated in Figure 11. It should be noted that Weber uses this system only to show chord roots; he does not use the figured-bass symbols to indicate inversions.

Figure 11.   *Use of Roman numeral chord symbols (Weber)*

Because of its foundation on observation of musical practice, Weber's harmonic theory was criticized by a few writers. As already noted, the reviewer for *Dwight's Journal* called Weber "a mere empiric." The Belgian theorist F. J. Fétis declared that Weber's "observation" approach had set harmonic theory back a hundred years, to its status in the time of the early figured-bass theorists.[39] In general, however, the *Theorie der Tonsetzkunst* met with popular approval. Even before the publication of Parts III and IV, Weber's terminology was being borrowed by Johann Gottlieb Werner (*Versuch einer kurzen und deutlichen Darstellung der Harmonielehre*, 1818) and Friedrich Schneider (*Elementarbuch der Harmonie und Tonsetzkunst*, 1820). For some time, in fact, there seems to have been the misconception that Schneider had invented the Roman-numeral system himself.[40] James Warner, in the Preface to the American edition of 1846, stated, "All things considered, no book of the kind holds so high a standing in Europe at the present time as does Godfrey Weber's *Theory of Musical Composition*."[41]

Of all Weber's followers, the one who contributed most to the spread of his theory was Ernst Friedrich Richter, professor of harmony at the Leipzig Conservatory. Richter's ability to give a clear, orderly presentation of practical harmonic theory is evident in his textbook, *Lehrbuch der Harmonie* (1857). The *Lehrbuch* became quite popular both in Germany and abroad; besides the American versions already mentioned, it appeared in translations into English (1864 for Great Britain), French (1884, 1911), Spanish (1892, 1928), Flemish (1896), Swedish, Russian, Polish, and Italian.[42]

Richter's book shows little of the argumentative character of Weber's writing. This is, of course, partly because such a tone would be out of place in the context of a textbook. Also, by 1857, the figured-bass treatises and stacked-third theories were fast disappearing from continental Europe, and the boundary between the domains of acoustical theory and practical harmony was more clearly recognized. Richter could even refer his readers to the work of his colleague Moritz Hauptmann (*Die Natur der Harmonik und Metrik*, 1853) for information on the acoustical basis of harmony.[43]

Richter fairly closely follows Weber's theory, making several additions and amplifications. In presenting the three essential harmonies of a key, he selects the tonic triad first, then looks for other triads that stand connected with it by "supporting themselves on one of its tones, yet which lie outside its tone-mass,"[44] thus discovering the dominant and subdominant triads. He also states that the major quality of the dominant triad in the minor key results from the raising of the triad's third to form a leading tone to the tonic, as in the harmonic progression V–I.[45]

Richter is more tolerant than Weber of the melodic forms of the minor scale. Although he presents the harmonic minor as the basic form of the scale, he realizes that the augmented second between the sixth and seventh scale degrees is melodically awkward. He therefore presents both types but is careful to state that the melodic forms "have no influence upon the harmonic formation in itself considered."[46]

Richter acknowledges as a legitimate harmony the augmented triad, which had been appearing more frequently in Romantic music.[47] The recognition of this triad makes it possible for Richter to construct a triad on every degree of the minor scale, as shown in Figure 12a.[48] Richter also admits the fully diminished seventh-chord as a "fundamental" chord type, and even acknowledges the major seventh-chord with the augmented fifth, thus enabling him to complete Weber's series of seventh-chords in the minor key, as shown at Figure 12*b*. To Weber's chord symbols Richter adds an apostrophe, indicating the augmented chords (e.g., III′, III′7).

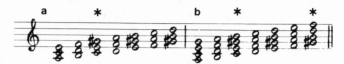

Figure 12. Richter, p. 64

Richter's presentation of the nonharmonic tones is more detailed than Weber's. Part II of the *Lehrbuch*, devoted to nonharmonic tones, treats not only the suspension but also the pedal tone, the passing tone, and the changing tone. Richter makes a distinction between pedal tone, which occurs in the lowest voice, and the "stationary tone," which appears in an upper voice.[49] He uses the term "changing tone" to refer both to the neighboring tone and the appoggiatura.[50] In discussing passing tones, he introduces the "harmonic by-tone," a chord tone which occurs accidentally within a passing-tone figuration.[51] In Figure 13, the tones marked with an asterisk are passing tones and the E, marked o, is a harmonic by-tone.

Figure 13. Richter, p. 128

From nonharmonic tones, Richter progresses to a remarkable discussion of "passing chords," which he defines as "those which in smaller parts of measures, after the manner of passing notes in several voices, appear as actual chord-formations, in the entrance and treatment of which, however, a manner is sometimes found deviating from the general rules of chord-connection."[52] Considered melodically, these formations are simply aggregates of unaccented nonharmonic tones; as they sound simultaneously, however, they accidentally form a fundamental chord. Because passing chords have less rhythmic weight, their harmonic significance is reduced, so that normal voice-leading rules may be somewhat relaxed for them. In Figure 14*a*, the chord marked with an asterisk is more readily perceived as a passing chord than as an inverted ii7 chord; consequently, the rule which would require the C, as seventh, to resolve downward is disregarded. At *b*, the appearance of the ⁶₄ chord, which Richter says is normally reserved for the precadential position, is admissible because of its passing character. Richter recognizes, then, that the influence of meter and rhythm on harmony aids in distinguishing between chords that have a definite function in the harmonic progression and chords that may be considered accumulations of passing and changing tones. "If this condition (the progression of voices by degrees) is fulfilled, then all chords can enter free; they will find explanation in the principal chord which immediately succeeds them."[53] The recognition that passing chords have relatively little meaning in basic harmonic progression is a contribution to the concept of harmonic function.

Figure 14.   Richter, p. 139

The final German theorist whose influence on American harmony must be considered is Immanuel Gottlob Faisst (1823–1894). Faisst was a cofounder (with Sigmund Lebert) of the Music Conservatory at Stuttgart, where he taught organ, theory, and composition prior to becoming its director in 1859.[54]

Faisst never published his system of harmony. In his "Preface" to Percy Goetschius's *The Material Used in Musical Composition*, Faisst mentions one of his students (not by name) who was later engaged as an instructor of harmony at the

Conservatory and who taught the course from the notes he had taken in Faisst's class.[55] Faisst's system was thus perpetuated at the Conservatory, where Goetschius encountered it. It was later adapted by Heinrich Lang, who published it under the title *Harmonielehre nach Immanuel Faisst*.[56]

Like other German theorists, Faisst regards the tonic, dominant, and subdominant triads as the principal harmonies of a key. He states that each represents an "area" of the tonality: "Of importance for the expression of a tonality are the triads I (tonic triad), V (dominant triad), and IV (subdominant triad) (I as the center, V as the higher area, and IV as the lower area of the tonality). These become the principal triads. The entire tonality is expressed in these principal triads."[57]

In discussing progressions between the principal triads, Faisst shows a remarkable awareness of the difference in effect between chord progressions involving root movements up a fifth and those in which the root descends a fifth: "The transition from I to V gives the operation a lifting and stimulating harmonic feeling. The opposite connection V I gives the operation a harmonic feeling of subsiding and relaxing, and is therefore appropriate to be used as the regular ending of a piece."[58] A similar sense of relaxation is observed in the progression from the tonic to the subdominant: "Here I to IV itself behaves as V to I, thus the succession I IV (with the cadence-like bass progression) produces a depressing and relaxing influence; this is frequently used to ornament the perfect cadence, with, of course, the return to I."[59] Thus Faisst acknowledges the feeling of resolution produced by the descending-fifth root movement.

Faisst designates as secondary triads the chords II, III, and VI in major keys and VI in minor (he acknowledges diminished and augmented triads, but is reluctant to treat them as independent chords). The tonal legitimacy of each of the secondary triads is dependent upon its identification with a principal triad:

> The secondary triads are called thus, because they seem less appropriate for the expression of the tonality. Yet they have their usual tonal significance when they operate as representatives of principal triads. Each of the consonant secondary triads now stands in near relation to the principal triad standing a minor third higher:

the VI in major and minor to the I,
the II in major to the IV,
the III in major to the V
in such manner, so that secondary triads readily serve as either representatives or follower-companions of the principal triads.[60]

Faisst, then, recognizes the similarity of the functions of the II and the IV chords, as well as the VI and the I. He admits, however, that the relation between the III and the V is not nearly as strong, stating that the usual function of the III is to harmonize the seventh scale degree in a descending melodic line.[61]

Faisst's treatment of second-inversion triads is noteworthy. Whereas Richter had permitted second-inversion triads only in precadential or passing contexts, Faisst distinguishes between "strong" and "weak" second-inversion triads. A "strong" second-inversion triad is one which stands adjacent to a chord whose bass note is the same as its own, such as the chords marked by an asterisk in Figure 15*a* and *b*. A weak second-inversion triad is one whose bass appears in the position of a passing tone, as shown in *c*.[62]

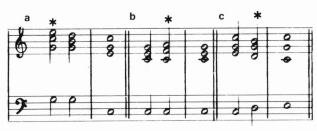

Figure 15. "Strong" and "weak" second-inversion triads (Faisst)

Faisst acknowledges dissonant chords on the dominant, supertonic, submediant, and mediant scale degrees. He treats at length the dissonant harmonies on the dominant and supertonic (called "changing-dominant"). His reason for replacing the principal subdominant harmony with that of the supertonic in this instance apparently lies in his observation of the inclination of dissonant chords to resolve by root-movements of descending fifths: "Every dissonant chord finds its regular resolution in a chord whose root stands a fifth lower or a fourth higher than that of the dissonant chord, so that the progression of the root delineates the natural, namely the cadence-like, root-movement."[63] Since the tendency of the II7 and II9 is to resolve to V, Faisst treats the IV7, whose goal is also V, as a II9 with an omitted root.[64] Similarly, he explains the chord on the leading tone as a dissonant dominant chord with the root omitted.[65] In any case, the concept of the dissonant chords progressing in root movements of descending fifths with the tonal center as their ultimate goal must have made a very strong impression on Goetschius, whose harmonic theory would be based primarily on this concept.

Faisst uses only uppercase Roman numerals to indicate chord roots. To indicate a chord in inversion, he supplements the Roman numeral with an arabic subscript, which indicates the ordinal number of the inversion. A tonic triad in first inversion is thus indicated I_1, or in second inversion I_2.[66] The arabic numerals indicating dissonances must be moved to a position above the Roman numeral, and the 0 indicating an omitted root is placed to the numeral's left (for example, $_0V_1^7$ represents a dominant seventh-chord in first inversion with an omitted root). This makes it possible for Faisst to indicate both the roots and the inversions of chords without the aid of a notated bass or figured-bass symbols (the *Harmonielehre* does not contain a single notated musical example). Faisst's "absolute" chord-symbol system would be used by Goetschius, who would convey it to the United States in his works.

The Victorian Theorists: Alfred Day, Rev. Sir F. A. Gore Ouseley, Ebenezer Prout

Although Gottfried Weber and his followers scorned it, the idea of using the harmonic series to construct and explain harmony engaged the theorists of Victorian England. The English theorists attempted to derive all the harmonic material in a given key from the natural harmonics of the tonic note, thereby proving the connection between harmony and nature. From its inception in England in 1845 to its culmination in the work of Ebenezer Prout, this theory was constantly being modified to correct problems of intonation. Although not entirely successful, the resulting system of harmonic theory was at least formidable.

The first English writer to propose such a system was Dr. Alfred Day (1810–1849), a London physician whose *A Treatise on Harmony* was written during his leisure time and published in 1845. In Part Two, Day enumerates the tones that can be derived from a harmonic series: "The harmonics from any given note (without taking the order in which they arise, but their practical use) are, major third, perfect fifth, minor seventh, minor or major ninth, eleventh, and minor or major thirteenth."[67] In a given key, Day constructs such a chord first on the tonic note, then on the dominant, and finally on the supertonic:

> The reason why the tonic, dominant and supertonic are chosen for roots is, because the harmonics in nature rise in the same manner; first the harmonics of any given note, then those of its fifth, or dominant, then those of the fifth of that dominant, being the second or supertonic of the original note. The reason why the harmonics of the next fifth are not used is, because that note itself is not a note of the diatonic scale, being a little too sharp (as the fifth of the supertonic) and can only be used as a part of a chromatic chord.[68]

In C major, the three natural harmonic entities appear as in Figure 16. Day considers these chords to include all the sounds of the key of C.

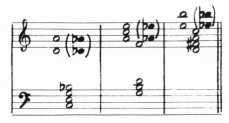

Figure 16.   Natural chords in C major (Day, p. 52)

There are several fallacies in Day's theory, notably those arising from the matter of intonation. The seventh harmonic partial, for example, is flatter in the harmonic series than it appears in the scale. In C major, the B-flat of the tonic root is slightly too flat, as is the F a seventh above the dominant, and the C generated by the supertonic is a bit lower than the original root C. Although these tones are only 63:64 flatter than they appear in the scale, this difference is noted by some of Day's followers.

The intonation problems with other notes are equally serious. The major ninth above the dominant is 80:81 too sharp; Day himself points this out when rejecting it as a possible root. The major thirteenth is 39:40 flatter than its counterpart in the major scale. The eleventh is 32:33 too sharp as it appears in the harmonic series; in fact, because this is a difference of nearly a quarter tone, Day omits it in the chords constructed on the tonic and supertonic.[69] He does, however, choose to use it in the chord on the dominant, apparently because he needs it for his explanation of the subdominant triad. It forms a glaring inconsistency with the tonic note.

Day's acoustical theory was modified somewhat by the Reverend Sir Frederick A. Gore Ouseley (1825–1889), professor of music at Oxford University, in his *Treatise on Harmony*, published in 1868. Ouseley, like Day, begins by constructing the harmonic series from a root, or "generator," as far as the sixteenth partial, but he notes the several pitches that are out of tune: "Now of these there are four marked X which are not only foreign to the key of C, but are *out of tune* in any key. Four others, marked ⊙, are merely repetitions of the major triad in an upper octave. . . . Only two remain, D and B, which we can make use of for our present purposes."[70] Ouseley next constructs the harmonic series from G, in which D becomes the third harmonic and B the fifth. However, in doing so he also admits the out-of-tune seventh, with a qualification:

X ⊙ ⊙ X ⊙ X X ⊙

Figure 17. Ouseley, p. 15

X

Figure 18. Ouseley, p. 20

Here it will be observed that every note belongs to the key of C till we come to the double-bar: and although the note marked X, is not perfectly in tune, yet we can substitute a really true F without materially disturbing our series of sounds . . . we get our residuum the chord G–B–D–F–A which is called the 'dominant chord of nature,' being based on the fifth of the key.[71]

The substitution of the "really true F" for the natural seventh led the Scottish theorist Matthew Shirlaw to dub this chord "the dominant chord of nature corrected by Ouseley."[72]

    Following Day's example, Ouseley also constructs a similar series on the supertonic. The supertonic is chosen as a root because it is "the one which affords new secondary harmonics the least remote from the tonic root."[73] Moreover, it is "produced by a square number, $3 \times 3 = 9$, and is therefore, the fifth of the fifth of the root."[74] In his search for this third root, Ouseley considers the seventh but rejects it as a possibility; due to its out-of-tuneness, it "produces intervals, every one of which would require the same great amount of alteration and tempering as is required in its own case."[75] Ouseley's rejection of the seventh as a root for this reason is inconsistent with his acceptance of it in his "dominant chord of nature."

    Ouseley admits the seventeenth and nineteenth harmonics of each root into the key, giving him the minor ninth and minor tenth above each root. This enables him to explain the tonic minor chord as being made up of the sixteenth, nineteenth, and twenty-fourth harmonics of the keynote.[76]

    The ultimate modification of Day's theory was made by Ebenezer Prout (1835–1909) in his treatise *Harmony, its Theory and Practice*, which was published concurrently in London and New York in 1889. Prout begins by using the keynote, C, to generate its harmonic series up to the twentieth term, then substitutes various secondary harmonics for the harmonics that are out of tune. The eleventh harmonic, for instance, which is approximately a quarter tone sharper than F, is discarded and replaced by the twenty-first, which is a secondary harmonic, the seventh of G, and is closer to being in tune: The ninth harmonic, D, may optionally be replaced by the seventeenth, D-flat. The thirteenth, which sounds somewhere between A-flat and A, is replaced either by the twenty-seventh, which is the ninth of the dominant, to obtain A, or by the fifty-first, which is the seventeenth of the dominant, to obtain A-flat. The process is then repeated using the dominant, G, and the supertonic, D, as roots.[77] The three chords appear in Figure 19.

Figure 19.   Prout, pp. 35–36

To critics, the most disconcerting feature of this theory is the seeming arbitrariness with which Prout sorts through the harmonic series and selects notes that suit his purposes. "Anyone is at liberty, if he so desires, to build up huge sound-combinations by means of adding thirds to one another; anyone may, from a harmonic series extended to the fifty-first term, pick out whatever sounds he may please, but why describe this as the science of harmony?"[78] Moreover, despite Prout's substitutions, the notes still are not in perfect tune. The seventh of each series is still 63:64 flatter than it appears in the key, because it is not "corrected." Each eleventh is similarly too flat, being the seventh harmonic of a secondary root. The thirteenth, on the other hand, is 80:81 sharper than its position in the scale.

In defense of such intonation problems, the Victorian theorists frequently cite equal temperament, which, after all, is an artificial, rather than a natural, phenomenon. George A. Macfarren, a follower of Day, states that the listener's ear has become so much accustomed to the tempered scale that it automatically accepts tempered notes as adjustments of natural pitches. "The minor seventh of nature is somewhat flatter and the eleventh somewhat sharper than the notes rendered in musical performance, which from custom the ear accepts as correct . . . it is an abnormal condition of the musical sense to tolerate, nay, to look for these qualified sevenths and elevenths."[79] According to Macfarren, then, the ear is capable of tolerating such notes as a tempered eleventh, which is "out of tune" by nearly a quarter of a tone with the natural eleventh.

The purpose of the English theorists' efforts at constructing huge chord formations on the tonic, dominant, and supertonic notes of a key was to explain every conceivable concordant and discordant harmony in that key in terms of one of these three chords. In this way, they attempted to demonstrate the origin of all tonal harmony in nature. According to Prout, for instance, the subdominant triad does not truly exist as a concord in a key, but is in fact formed by the seventh, ninth, and eleventh of the dominant chord.[80] Similarly, the triad on the sixth degree of the scale is actually a dominant thirteenth discord, with the root, third, fifth, and seventh omitted.[81] The minor seventh chord on the supertonic is explained by Ouseley as being derived from two roots, or "generators": the third of the chord is actually the seventh of the dominant, while the root, fifth, and seventh are generated by the supertonic.[82] Prout explains the same chord as simply the fifth, seventh, ninth, and eleventh of the dominant.[83]

The English theorists give extensive rules pertaining to the use of seventh-, ninth-, eleventh-, and thirteenth-chords. These rules include instructions for the proper resolution of each note in the discord, as well as recommendations for omissions of notes. Day's work contains forty-nine pages of such rules. Ouseley's treatise devotes twenty-five pages to the chords of the dominant seventh and dominant major ninth and another nine pages to the dominant minor ninth-chord. Ouseley explains how to resolve each chord member properly and which notes to double or omit in each inversion, even in the inversions which he admits are not generally used. In his discussion of the dominant major ninth, for example, he says that, "the fourth inversion is crude and harsh, and should be avoided." Having banned it, he continues,

> In it the ninth is in the bass; consequently its natural resolution is into the second inversion of the tonic triad . . . the ninth being below the fifth, no consecutive fifths are produced, and therefore the fifth may either ascend or descend . . . it is almost always necessary to leave out the octave of the root; indeed, the chord is almost never seen in its complete form on account of its extreme harshness. The fifth may also be omitted, and even the seventh and the leading note, though these last two omissions almost divest the chord of its dominant character: whichever of these two is omitted, therefore, the other must always be retained.[84]

Certainly this is a lot of attention to devote to an inversion which is to be avoided in the first place.

Ebenezer Prout is even more loquacious on the topic of discords, devoting sixty-two pages, or almost a quarter of the treatise, to the use of seventh- , ninth- , eleventh- , and thirteenth-chords. Most of Prout's musical illustrations are passages from existing works, rather than four-part examples for students' imitation, and it is instructive to examine a few of his analyses.

In Figure 20, Prout identifies the chord marked with an asterisk as a supertonic minor ninth-chord in which the root, D, and the fifth, A, are omitted.[85] The excerpt by Schubert in Figure 21 illustrates a supertonic major ninth-chord (marked with an asterisk) resolving to a dominant eleventh-chord with the root and third omitted (marked with a double asterisk).[86] Prout analyzes the chord marked with an asterisk in Figure 22 as a dominant eleventh-chord, which resolves to a supertonic minor ninth-chord with an omitted root on the second beat of the measure, before reaching the tonic harmony.[87] Prout's analysis, shown in Figure 22, especially shows how easily the terms "tonic," "dominant," and "supertonic" lose their functional implications in the English theory. The three terms are obviously intended more to identify the acoustical origins of chords than to explain how they behave in a harmonic progression.

Figure 20. Mozart, Sonata in C minor *(Prout, p. 157)*

Figure 21. Schubert, Sonata, Op. 154 *(Prout, p. 155)*

Figure 22.   Beethoven, Sonata, Op. 14, no. 2 (Prout, p. 172)

According to Prout—and all the English theorists, for that matter—many chords that appear to be chromatic are really portions of the three natural chords, but spelled enharmonically. If one were to spell the chromatic scale of C using only the notes in the three natural chord-formations, all the nondiatonic notes would appear as flattened steps except for the raised fourth, which is generated by the supertonic. The correct spelling of the chromatic scale according to Prout is shown in Figure 23.[88] Raised scale degrees other than the fourth are nothing more than attempts by composers to simplify the appearance of the music; they are not theoretically correct. Prout explains that the chord marked with an asterisk in Figure 24 is actually a dominant minor thirteenth-chord with the fifth, seventh, and ninth omitted. The thirteenth, represented by B-natural, should actually be spelled C-flat.[89] In an example by Auber (see Figure 25), the chord marked with an asterisk is analyzed in D major as the last inversion of a dominant major thirteenth-chord with a minor ninth, which Auber wrote as A-sharp but which properly would be spelled B-flat. The root, fifth, seventh, and eleventh are omitted.[90]

Figure 23.   The chromatic scale (Prout, p. 121)

Only rarely is an example found of a complete thirteenth-chord, such as the first chord of the last movement of Beethoven's Ninth Symphony, shown in Figure 26. Prout analyzes this as a dominant minor thirteenth-chord in sixth inversion. As an afterthought, however, he remarks that "it is only right to add that this combination may also be explained as a

Figure 24. Beethoven, Sonata, *Op. 30, no. 2 (Prout, p. 154)*

Figure 25. Auber, Le Dieu et la Bayadère *(Prout, p. 155)*

Figure 26. Beethoven, Symphony No. 9, *Op. 125 (Prout, p. 192)*

tonic chord with the notes of the dominant harmony sounded over it as auxiliary notes."[91]

The English theorists explain some chords as having double roots. Day, Ouseley, and Prout all give just such an explanation for the chords of the augmented sixth.[92] In the French augmented sixth-chord, for instance, the upper three notes are all generated by the supertonic, while the lowest note is the minor ninth of the dominant, which resolves to its own root, as shown in Figure 27. The German and Italian sixths are similarly analyzed. Ouseley also explains the Neapolitan sixth-chord as having two roots. In the cadence in Figure 28, the chord marked with an asterisk is, according to Ouseley, produced by the seventh and minor ninth of the dominant (F and A-flat) and the minor ninth of the tonic (D-flat). Since the two roots, C and G, are respectively the dominant and supertonic of F, Ouseley considers the chord to represent a transient modulation to the subdominant, "and thus we see a connection between this cadence and the plagal cadence."[93]

Figure 27. The French augmented sixth-chord

Figure 28. Ouseley, p. 163

There are only minor discrepancies among the English theorists' discussions of nonharmonic tones. Ouseley distinguishes between a suspension, which resolves downward, and a retardation, which resolves upward.[94] Prout considers that suspensions may resolve either downward or upward.[95] Prout also makes several distinctions not made by Ouseley between suspensions and members of discords. In Figure 29 the E in *a* is a suspended note because it resolves during the chord above which it is suspended. At *b* the E is actually the ninth of a chord because it does not resolve until the next chord sounds. Suspensions may also be identified by means of the rules regarding omissions of notes from the discords.[96] For instance, the seventh must always be present in a minor ninth-chord in root position; hence, the F in Figure 30 is not a member of the chord and must therefore be considered a suspension. It would be interesting to know what Prout would have done with the F from Richter's *Lehrbuch*, shown in Figure 31.[97] The F, according to Prout's rules, can be neither a ninth (since there is no seventh) nor a suspension (since it does not resolve until the next chord sounds).

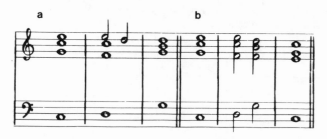

Figure 29.   *Distinction between suspension and chord ninth (Prout)*

Figure 30.   *Suspension (Prout)*

Figure 31.   *Suspension (Richter,* Manual of Harmony, *p. 118)*

Other nonharmonic types mentioned are the pedal tone, the passing tone, and the auxiliary tone. Both Ouseley and Prout adopt a rule that lower auxiliary tones must neighbor the principal note by a semitone, although Prout makes an exception for an auxiliary beneath the third of a chord.[98] Prout also states that an auxiliary note may resolve by leaping a third—and occasionally farther[99]—which, of course, forms the escape tone. Ouseley defines the appoggiatura simply as an accented auxiliary tone, but his example shows it being approached by a leap.[100] In general, the English theorists used the term *auxiliary* loosely, referring to any sort of nonharmonic tone except the suspension and the pedal tone.

The English theorists deal with modulation in various ways. Ouseley is rather vague on the subject. Although he never defines modulation precisely, he uses the term constantly to refer not only to chromatic harmonies but also to diatonic events. For instance, he considers the ascending major scale to modulate to its subdominant as it passes through the fourth, fifth, and sixth degrees.[101] He does not require that the new key be established after a modulation but gives many examples of sequential "modulation," such as Figure 32, in which only one chord is required to define each key.[102]

Figure 32.   Ouseley, p. 58

Prout is more definite about modulation. He states emphatically that in a modulation the chord containing the new accidental must be followed by other chords in the same key, as "no single chord can ever define a key. . . . To determine any key, at least two chords, and sometimes more, must be regarded in their relationship to one another."[103] In Figure 33, then, the passage in *a* has modulated to G major, while *b* remains in C major throughout. The D-major chord in *b* is, of course, explainable as a supertonic discord.

Prout also distinguishes between nearly related keys and remote keys. Using Helmholtz's definition of consonance (in which two notes are said to be consonant if they have at least one strong harmonic partial in common), he states that "Two keys

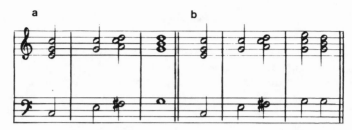

Figure 33. Distinction between a modulation and an altered chord (Prout)

are said to be related to one another when their tonics are consonant, and the more perfect the consonance, the nearer the relationship."[104] The two most nearly related keys to C are therefore F and G major, whose tonics each lie a fifth from C. The keys whose tonics lie a third or sixth from C are "also related, but more distantly." However, Prout also identifies the relative minor of the original key as a near relative on the strength of the great number of notes the two scales have in common, although he confesses that they have no connection by his acoustical theory.[105] He then extends the relationship to the relative minors of the two nearly related major keys, so that any major key has five nearly related keys (see Figure 34).

| F major | C MAJOR | G major |
| D minor | A minor | E minor |

Figure 34. Table of nearly related keys (Prout, p. 102)

The difficulty in such an identification of key relationships lies in its double explanation. According to the standard of consonance between tonic notes, the keys of E, E-flat, A, and A-flat major are somewhat related to C, but the keys of D and B-flat, whose tonics are a major second from C, are absolutely unrelated. However, Prout acknowledges only the harmonic form of the minor scale. Therefore, the keys of D minor and E minor, which he admits as near relatives of C major, have only five notes in common with C.[106] By this standard, D major and B-flat major should also be admitted, since they also each have five notes in common with the C major scale; alternately, D minor should be rejected, since its tonic lies a major second from that of C.

The influence of the system of tonic, dominant, and supertonic "generators" is reflected in Prout's closing remark concerning key relationships:

> As a general rule, a modulation to the dominant side of the tonic—that is, to a key containing more sharps, or fewer flats—is to be preferred to one to the subdominant side—that is, a key having more flats or fewer sharps. The reason of this is that the dominant is a key generated out of the tonic, as also are other keys with more sharps than itself. When, therefore, we modulate into one of these keys, the tonic still maintains its position as the source of whence the whole music springs. But the tonic itself is a derivative of keys having more flats than itself—e.g., C is the dominant of F, and the mediant of A-flat; and when we modulate into one of these keys the original tonic sinks into a subordinate position as a *derived* key. If, for instance, we modulate from C to F and make a long stay in the latter key, we shall when we return to C most likely get the mental impression, not of returning to the key of the tonic, but of going into a dominant key. For this reason the feeling of the key is much more readily disturbed and much sooner obliterated by a modulation to the subdominant side of the key than to the dominant side.[107]

The entire system of Victorian theory, based on the generation of all chords in a key from the harmonic partials of its tonic, was abandoned in England in 1901, when the sixteenth edition of Prout's *Harmony, its Theory and Practice* appeared. This edition has rightly been described as a "new work on harmony."[108] In it, Prout, who had brought Day's acoustical theory of "generators" to its culmination, renounces the entire business. "First and foremost among these [revisions] is the virtual abandonment of the harmonic series as the basis on which the system is founded. Further investigation and thought have convinced the author that the practical objections to the derivation of the higher discords—the ninths, elevenths, and thirteenths—from the natural series of upper partials were far greater than he realized in first writing the volume."[109] In this edition Prout relegates his explanation of the harmonic series to an appendix and constructs the scales, both major and minor, from the notes of the tonic, dominant, and subdominant triads, much as Weber had done. Prout also makes use of Weber's system of Roman numerals in his harmonic analyses (previously, the English had not done so, since they had admitted only three fundamental roots), and he greatly reduces the explanations of the ninth-, eleventh- , and thirteenth-chords.

By 1901, however, Victorian concepts of harmony had already affected the development of harmonic theory in the United States. By then Percy Goetschius's treatise *The Materials Used in Musical Composition* had been in print in the United States for twelve years. Although Goetschius's acoustical basis was different, the structure of his practical harmonic theory exhibited some remarkable similarities to the English system.

2
Percy Goetschius

Percy Goetschius is rightly regarded as the father of American theory. As a teacher and an author of works on harmony, counterpoint, and musical form, he exerted a tremendous influence on the work of subsequent American theorists, an influence which has survived to the present day. George T. Jones, in examining Goetschius's *Material Used in Musical Composition*, remarks, "Many of the newer theory texts owe a great deal to Goetschius, even though the present authors may be unaware of their indebtedness. Important ideas . . . have been subtly transmitted by this work from the 1880's when the first edition appeared, through many teacher-pupil generations, down to the present day."[1]

A brief biography of Goetschius will suffice here.[2] Born in 1853 in Paterson, New Jersey, Percy Goetschius showed an early aptitude for music. By the time he was ten years old he had taught himself to play the flute and the piano. Mr. U. C. Hill, a friend of Goetschius's father, encouraged the boy to develop his musical talents further. Finally, in 1873, Goetschius abandoned his father's plan that he become a civil engineer and sailed to Europe to study music.

At Stuttgart Goetschius studied composition and theory with Immanuel Faisst, who was evidently impressed with Goetschius's ability. After Goetschius had completed the usual three-year conservatory course in a year and a half, he began teaching as a substitute for Faisst, whose schedule of organ recitals and music festivals was becoming increasingly hectic. In

1876 Goetschius was given charge of the English-speaking classes at the Stuttgart Conservatory. In 1882 he published *The Material Used in Musical Composition*, an adaptation of Faisst's notes for use by the English-speaking students at the Conservatory. In 1889 the book was published in the United States by G. Schirmer.

Goetschius returned to the United States in 1889 and accepted a teaching position at Syracuse University. In 1892 he resigned in order to accept a more attractive position at the New England Conservatory. In the same year *The Theory and Practice of Tone-Relations* was published by G. Schirmer. Goetschius taught at the New England Conservatory only until 1896, when he resigned because of differences with the Conservatory director, Carl Faelten, and retired to a career of private teaching in the Boston area. It was during this retirement that his series of books on counterpoint and musical form began to appear, as well as the first revision of *The Theory and Practice of Tone-Relations*.

In 1904 Frank Damrosch, who was then organizing the Institute of Musical Art in New York, invited Goetschius to head the new school's theory department. Goetschius accepted the position and remained at the Institute for twenty years. Upon his retirement he moved to Manchester, New Hampshire, where he spent the rest of his life writing books and articles on music. He died in 1943, a few months after his ninetieth birthday.

During his life Goetschius produced a formidable battery of treatises and textbooks on music. Besides the two harmony books, *The Material Used in Musical Composition* (1882) and *The Theory and Practice of Tone-Relations* (1892), he wrote: *The Homophonic Forms of Musical Composition* (1898), *Exercises in Melody-Writing* (1900), *Counterpoint* (1902), *Lessons on Musical Form* (1904), *The Larger Forms of Musical Composition* (1915), *Masters of the Symphony* (1929), *Music Theory for Piano Students* (with C. G. Hamilton, 1930), *The Structure of Music* (1934), and others.

A criticism frequently leveled at Goetschius's work is that he does not account sufficiently for developments taking place in the music of the late nineteenth and early twentieth centuries. Goetschius's reluctance to deal with these modern developments may be attributed to his personal dislike of the music of the late Romantic era. George Wedge recalls that to Goetschius, "Brahms was the last word; Strauss and Debussy were 'possible.' "[3] Goetschius's attitude is reflected in his textbooks; examples from late Romantic music appear occasionally in his writing, but usually only as illustrations of exceptional, rather than standard, procedures. "The publication dates of [Goetschius's] books (1882–1934) span a period of over fifty years, years during which changes and developments in musical technique approached the revolutionary stage, but none of this appears in these texts. The music which interested Goetschius and which he wanted his pupils to know and imitate was that of the classic-romantic era, and he wrote his books accordingly."[4]

Another criticism of Goetschius's writing is that despite the high level of organization (or perhaps because of it) the material is presented in extremely complicated detail. "The literary style of the books reveals the man—meticulous, precise, tending toward the complicated and didactic."[5] Daniel Gregory Mason suggests that "maybe his published textbooks do not quite do him justice. His tendency in writing was to load his general principles down with such masses of detail as they could hardly penetrate. In reading one is apt to become bewildered, and lose sight of the law behind the cloud of rules."[6]

The inclination toward almost tiresome detail is evident in his two books on harmony. The format of chapters of numbered paragraphs is obviously borrowed from the Victorian authors, and cross-references to paragraphs and illustrations occur constantly. Part-writing rules are frequently given amid blizzards of qualifications, recommendations, exceptions, and descriptions of irregular procedures. The exposition of nonharmonic tones in particular suffers from an excess of exceptions and qualifications.

The unique features of Goetschius's theory of harmony first appeared in the early American editions of *The Material Used in Musical Composition* and remained uniform through all subsequent revisions of this work, as well as in *The Theory and Practice of Tone-Relations*. It should be noted that the Stuttgart (1882) version of the *Material Used in Musical Composition* does not contain many of Goetschius's unique ideas; in this version, for instance, Goetschius presents the Rameau-Weber explanation of the scale, namely, that it is a compilation of the notes of the principal triads I, IV, and V. Mother Carroll offers the conjecture that Goetschius used this explanation because he was conscious of Faisst's watchful eye.[7] In any case, this explanation of the scale's origin is replaced in American editions by Goetschius's own theory, which he calls "tone-relations" and which forms the basis of his entire system of harmony.

The Theory of Tone-Relations

The initial difference between Goetschius's theory and the contemporary European systems of harmony lies in his attitude toward the relationship of harmony to melody. In the writings of the German and the British theorists, there was no doubt that melody, represented by the scale, is a product of harmony. It has been seen that the German theorists explained the major and harmonic minor scales as linear arrangements of the notes of the tonic, dominant, and subdominant triads. The Victorian theorists similarly constructed their harmonic entities at the outset, only afterwards using the notes of their "natural" chords to form scales. In fact, the sole nineteenth-century theorist who disagreed with the concept that melody arises from harmony was the Belgian writer F. J. Fétis, who used the scale as the basis of his system.

Goetschius's system does not use either harmony or melody as the basis of each other. Rather, both melody and harmony arise simultaneously from the principle that Goetschius calls "tone-relations": "Every combination, every progression, every obligation is based upon and defined by the correlation of tones. A solitary tone has (ordinarily) no more meaning than a single letter or character of speech has; both acquire a signification only upon being associated with other characters, whereby a relationship is established, involving mutual obligations and evolving action."[8]

The acoustic basis of Goetschius's theory of tone-relations is the interval of the fifth. Beginning with the customary illustration of a string vibrating 261 times per second to produce C, Goetschius discovers that another string, half the length of the first, vibrates twice as fast, or 522 times per second, sounding the C one octave higher than the original pitch. The interval of the octave, then, may be represented by the proportion 1:2. However, Goetschius states that "the octave is of no great use in active Harmony, as it merely alters the register of what is practically the same tone—so complete is the agreement."[9] Goetschius proceeds to the next simplest string division and its corresponding proportion, 2:3, which produces the fifth. He considers this fifth to be of paramount importance because it produces a tone which is *not* an octave transposition of the original pitch: "The perfect fifth is of the greatest significance in Harmony, as it represents the simplest mathematical proportion and consequently the most intimate relation which can exist between actually different tones, and therefore constitutes the basis of all tone-combination."[10] He declares the fifth to be the standard of measurement in harmony and names it "the Harmonic Degree."

Having obtained the fifth, Goetschius uses it in a novel manner to construct his system of tone-relations. He begins with the tonic note C and projects a succession of fifths upward as far as B, and downward once, to F, to produce the configuration shown in Figure 35. Goetschius names this configuration the "Natural Scale" and notes that if its members are arranged within the compass of the octave above the tonic note they form the diatonic major scale.[11] The fifth, then, is shown to be the basis of the melodic aspect of tone-relations.

Figure 35. The "Natural Scale"

Goetschius considers his method of constructing the scale to be original; in fact, he points it out in the "Preface" of *The Material Used in Musical Composition* as one of the unique elements of his theory.[12] It is true that this system is quite different from anything proposed by Goetschius's European contemporaries. What Goetschius actually presents, however, is by no means new in the history of music. It coincides exactly with the ancient Pythagorean system of tuning, which was used in classical Greece and throughout the Middle Ages.

Because the European theorists of the eighteenth and nineteenth centuries had considered harmony to precede melody, they had used as a standard the scale produced by just intonation, which is based upon the formation of the major triads from the first five harmonics of their roots. A C major scale in just intonation includes an E which stands above C by a major third of the proportion 4:5. The A is situated a similar major third above the F, and the B similarly above G. Compared with a C major scale in just intonation, Goetschius's scale contains an A, an E, and a B which are too sharp. Goetschius's major third from C to E is of the proportion $2:3 \times 2:3 \times 2:3 \times 2:3 = 81$, or reduced to within the same octave, 64:81. This is sharper by a Pythagorean comma, 80:81, than the third 4:5 (64:80) in just intonation. The comparison is shown in Figure 36. The A and the B of Goetschius's scale are also each sharper by a comma than their counterparts in just intonation.

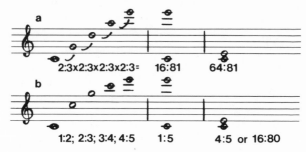

Figure 36.   *Comparison of major third in just intonation with Goetschius's major third*

Goetschius's scale fares somewhat better when compared with the system of equal temperament, which became standard in Europe and the United States by the middle of the nineteenth century.[13] A tempered fifth is represented approximately by the proportion 293:439, or 700 cents,[14] whereas the natural fifth, 2:3, measures 702 cents. The difference of two cents is considered to be imperceptible. In Goetschius's scale, then, the G is two cents sharper than that of the tempered scale, the D is four cents sharper, and so on, each fifth-progression gaining two cents. The F is two cents too flat. Although every note but the keynote is thus slightly out of tune, the difference is much smaller than that between Goetschius's scale and that of just intonation. The note B, the one most seriously out of tune with its tempered counterpart, differs from the tempered B by only ten cents. Since the system of equal temperament was well established by 1889, Goetschius might easily have remarked upon the difference between the natural and the tempered fifths.

After discovering the fifth, Goetschius proceeds to derive other consonant intervals from the harmonic series. He defines the consonant intervals as those having the proportions 1:2, 2:3, 3:4, 4:5, and 5:6, and he uses these consonances to construct his chords.[15] Goetschius's chords are therefore of the same proportions as those of just intonation, and their intervals disagree accordingly with the intervals produced by his scale. The E in Goetschius's C major triad, for instance, is not the same E that was reached by fifths in his natural scale but is flatter by a comma. The A in the F major triad and the B in the G major triad are similarly flatter than their counterparts in his scale.

In constructing his natural scale, Goetschius realizes that the series of fifths might be projected upward infinitely. In order to limit the constituency of the key, he adopts the following rule: "A new higher perfect fifth is associated with each member last found until a tone is reached which would contradict the lowest one."[16] The progression upward must end at B because the next note, F-sharp, would contradict the F-natural a fifth below C.

By presenting the choice between F and F-sharp, Goetschius calls into question the legitimacy of the inclusion of the note a fifth below the tonic. If the progression of fifths is to be upward from the tonic, what is the reason for the single exception of the subdominant? Why not continue upward and use F-sharp instead? The F at the bottom of the series is not produced by the C, but rather produces it. Goetschius's reason for preferring F-natural is that it lies only one harmonic degree from the tonic and is therefore more closely related to it than is F-sharp.[17] By this standard, however, it is possible also to include B-flat in the key of C, since B-flat, the secondary subdominant, is more closely related by fifths to C than is B-natural.

Goetschius realizes that the subdominant note represents an inconsistency in his system, and he takes great pains to justify its precedence over F-sharp. He argues that F-sharp is excluded because it "conflicts with the Keynote itself,"[18] presumably because it forms the dissonant augmented fourth with C. However, D and B, which also form dissonant intervals with C, are nonetheless admitted into the key. Perhaps Goetschius's most satisfactory argument is that the scale of C, assuming F rather than F-sharp, may be divided into two tetrachords which have identical arrangements of whole tones and semitones.[19]

Goetschius's difficulty in accounting for the F below the tonic C is nothing more than a manifestation of the "subdominant problem," which has frustrated theorists since the time of Rameau. A note used as a "root" produces upper partials to infinity but does not project a similar series downward. There is thus no acoustical justification for the note a fifth below the tonic, nor for the chord built upon it. The Victorian English theorists realized this;[20] it was their reason for resorting to the upper partials of the dominant in order to explain the subdominant. The German theorists, on the other hand, recognized that although the subdominant is elusive acoustically, it is an established fact of musical practice and cannot be ignored. They could account successfully for it as the antipode of the dominant only by abandoning any serious attempt at a realistic acoustic explanation.

The subdominant, real or not, is assigned an important position in Goetschius's rank of scale tones. Goetschius designates as the three "principal" notes of the scale the tonic, the dominant, and the subdominant, observing that the last two are each one harmonic degree distant from the tonic. The second-scale degree, though a subordinate note, is nonetheless important as the dominant of the dominant; Goetschius calls it the "second-dominant" because "it transfers the relationship of Tonic-Dominant to the Dominant itself."[21] For this reason he also refers to it by Faisst's term, "changing dominant." Of the remaining subordinate degrees, the mediant and submediant are given their customary explanation, that is, that they are "halfway" points between the tonic and the other two principal tones; and the leading tone tends upward to the tonic. The entire set of scale-degree relations is shown in Figure 37. From Figure 37 it may be seen that Goetschius attempts to adopt both the German and the English procedures. The designation of tonic, dominant, and subdominant as the three

principal members of a key (Figure 37a) forms the skeleton of the
system that Weber borrowed from Rameau and subsequent
German theorists promoted. At the same time, the designation
of the second-scale degree as the "second-dominant" is reminiscent not only of Faisst's system but also of the theory proposed
by Alfred Day and his followers. The second dominant is to play
an important part in Goetschius's theory of harmonic progression.

Figure 37.   Relations of scale degrees (Goetschius, Material Used, *p. 4)*

Goetschius classifies the degrees of the scale as either
melodically "active" or "inactive." The first-scale degree, the
tonic, has as its chief characteristic a sense of repose. Sharing this
feeling of repose with it are its third and fifth, which are produced
by its first five harmonics. The first, third, and fifth scale degrees
are therefore "inactive" tones. The others are "active," and each
must resolve to one of the inactive tones in order to satisfy the
ear.[22] The natural tendency of the seventh step is to lead upward
to the tonic. Similarly, the sixth degree inclines to the fifth, the
fourth to the third, and the second to either the first or the third.
Goetschius qualifies this classification by stating that melodic or
harmonic factors may alter the active or inactive status of a note.
Thus, in Figure 38a, the tendency of the leading tone to resolve
upward is overridden by the general melodic impetus downward.
At *b* the C loses its inactive quality because it is a member of a
dissonance.[23] The concept of melodically active and inactive
tones exerts an influence on harmony at several points in
Goetschius's theory.

Figure 38.   Goetschius, Material Used, *p. 6*

Diatonic Harmony; Theory of Harmonic Progression

Although the fifth, shown acoustically to be a consonant interval, is present in Goetschius's major and minor harmonies, its primary harmonic purpose is not the construction of chords. In this respect Goetschius's acoustical theory differs radically from that of the Victorian English theorists, who constructed only single chords from the harmonic series of each "generator." Goetschius uses the result of his acoustical research—the fifth, or "harmonic degree"—to define natural movement from one chord to another. By combining acoustical procedure with Faisst's concept of chord movement, Goetschius presents a unique and important theory of harmonic progression.

Goetschius begins by establishing the tonic, dominant, and subdominant triads as the principal harmonies of a key: "The quality of a chord is defined by the distance of its root from the tonic in harmonic degrees. This determines the extent to which it supports and confirms the key, and is also a test of its frequency and recognizability."[24] Thus the selection of the dominant and subdominant triads is justified; the root of each lies only one harmonic degree distant from the tonic. "The Tonic Triad and its two nearest relatives, the Dominant and the Subdominant Triads, are the principal chords of the key, and represent the three essential elements of harmony, among which the other three triads, (the Two, the Six, and the Three), called Subordinate chords, are only interspersed occasionally for the sake of variety, contrast, and embellishment."[25] The three principal triads are said to represent three classes of harmony: the Tonic Class, the Dominant Class (or First nontonic class of chords), and Subdominant (or Second) Class.[26]

In the "Preface" to *The Material Used in Musical Composition* Goetschius lays claim to the originality of his treatment of the subordinate triads.[27] His explanation of these triads, however, closely resembles that of Faisst:

> These three triads should not be regarded as entirely new and independent Harmonies, but merely as new forms of the Principal Triads. Aside from the relation which they bear to each other and to their Tonic there also exists an intimate and significant relationship between the separate Subordinate and Principal triads. Each Subordinate Triad alone is an accessory to one particular Principal

Triad, in the connection commonly known as "Relative" major and minor. Namely: the accessory of the I is the VI; the accessory of the IV is the II, and that of the V is the III.[28]

Goetschius is able to define the class, and consequently the function, of each subordinate triad in terms of the principal triad with which it is associated. "To its own Principal Triad each subordinate triad is closely related, usually acting as substitute for it and deducing most of its harmonic regulations from those of its Relative. Hence they are to be regarded as joint representatives of the same harmonic Class or Element."[29] He states that the strength of the relationship between each principal triad and its subordinate is determined by the distance of the subordinate triad in harmonic degrees from the tonic.[30] Thus, the II, which lies two harmonic degrees from the tonic, is related quite strongly to its relative major triad IV, whereas the VI has a slightly weaker relationship with its relative I, because the VI lies three degrees from the tonic. The III is the most tenuous: "This chord lies most remote from the Tonic centre, and is therefore the weakest, least frequent, and most embarrassing of all the Triads."[31] The relationships between the principal and subordinate triads is shown in Figure 39.

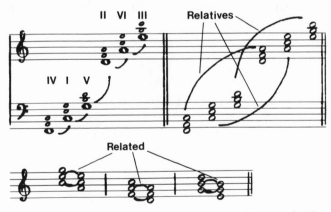

Figure 39.   *Relationships between principal and subordinate triads (Goetschius, Material Used, p. 40)*

The connection of the principal triads reveals that root movements upward in harmonic degrees do not produce the same effect as movements downward. In discussing the connection of the tonic and dominant triads, Goetschius, like Faisst, notes the difference in effect between ascending and descending root progressions in fifths. From this observation Goetschius deduces an important law:

> Although the chords I and V stand each in the relation of a Harmonic Degree to the other, it does not follow that their connection is equally natural either way. The natural arrangement of Chord-Roots *above* the Tonic (with one apparent exception accounted for later on) as seen in Example 24,[32] proves that their inclination must be *downwards* in Harmonic Degrees, in order to reach the Tonic, in which their obligations are fulfilled. Consequently, the succession V-I is more natural than I-V.[33]

Thus the concept of progression of roots downward in fifths toward the tonic center is introduced. It is to become the ruling principle of Goetschius's entire theory of chord progression.

The introduction of the subdominant triad into Goetschius's system presents difficulties. Goetschius notes that the relationship between I and IV is that of one harmonic degree, as is V and I, and that the root movement down a fifth from I to IV coincides with the natural downward progression of roots. This observation appears to lend support to the argument that the subdominant tends to usurp the function of the tonic; if the natural progression is downward in fifths, it should lead not only from the dominant to the tonic but also onward to the subdominant. Here Goetschius is able to make use of his distinction between active and inactive scale degrees; both the root and the third of the subdominant triad are active tones which lead downward to the third and fifth of the tonic triad.[34] The connection from the subdominant to the dominant is more difficult to explain, although it is a common progression in musical practice. In this progression the root movement is two harmonic degrees, one of them away from the tonic center. Goetschius does not explain this difficulty immediately. He does hint at the ultimate explanation, however, by making a somewhat alarming statement about the subdominant: "This is not the fundamental representative of the Second Class of non-tonic Chords, as will be seen."[35]

Goetschius's explanation of the minor scale is reminiscent of German procedure. Although the upward projection of fifths from the tonic yields a major scale, it does not similarly produce a minor scale. He concludes that the minor scale is a synthetic, not a natural, phenomenon. "The so-called 'Minor' scale is a modification of the 'Natural' or 'Major' scale, and may therefore be called an 'Artificial' scale."[36] The minor scale is formed by lowering the third of each of the principal triads, producing the arrangement shown in Figure 40. In minor, then, the basic form of the scale appears to arise from the harmony. Goetschius realizes that the Aeolian minor scale thus produced has a theoretical use: it demonstrates the minor key signature. In order to make the scale more useful melodically and harmonically, the active seventh degree is raised to a semitone beneath its destination, the tonic, as in Figure 41. He shows no compunction about making this alteration, since the minor scale is not a natural form anyway: "This minor scale, being only an 'artificial' scale in any case, submits readily to an ulterior modification by which the Leading-tone maintains its half-step proximity to the Tonic, and the Dominant Triad remains a major Chord, as in Major."[37] Goetschius states that melodic considerations may produce other forms of the minor scale. Modifications can easily be made because of the scale's artificiality.

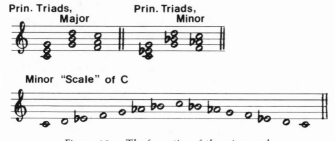

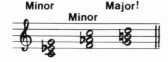

Figure 40. The formation of the minor scale

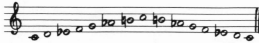

Figure 41. The minor scale with adjusted leading-tone

In his exposition of inverted triads, Goetschius introduces the "absolute" chord symbols invented by Faisst (e.g., I_1, I_2).[38] He also employs the traditional figured-bass symbols 6 and $\frac{6}{4}$ independently of the Roman numerals. His treatment of the second-inversion triads amplifies Faisst's "strong" and "weak" designations. According to Goetschius, a second-inversion triad may be used in any of three circumstances, shown in Figure 42a adjacent to a chord with the same bass note; b adjacent to a chord with the same root; or c adjacent to a chord on the next higher or lower bass note.

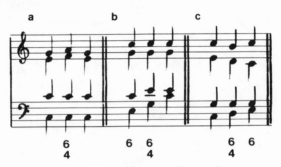

Figure 42. The three possible uses of the second-inversion triad

Goetschius's theory of natural chord progression comes to maturity when he discusses discords. He admits four positions of discords: on the dominant (First Class), on the supertonic (Second Class), on the submediant (Third Class), and on the mediant (Fourth Class). He states explicitly that there can be no discord in the tonic class; the chief characteristic of the tonic is its sense of repose, which would be lost if the tonic chord were to be alloyed with a dissonance.[39] The four classes of discords are rooted on successive harmonic degrees of the natural scale. Each discord resolves naturally to the harmony on the root a fifth below its own. Goetschius states that, since the discords of the Third and Fourth classes are rooted on the notes most remote in harmonic degrees from the tonic, they are "extremely rare, and scarcely maintain any appreciable connection with their key."[40] Thus he concludes that "the Tonic Class (exclusively consonant) and the First and Second Classes (both consonant and dissonant) represent together virtually the three

Elements of the whole System of Harmony."[41] The positions of the discords may be seen in Figure 43.

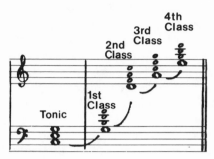

Figure 43.   Positions of discords

The possible dissonances in any of the nontonic classes are the seventh and ninth. Goetschius does not admit any eleventh- or thirteenth-chords: "To such tone-combinations as these, which extend beyond five tones and contain an undue proportion of Dissonances . . . a place is assigned among the so-called Inharmonic Elements, where they can be much more simply and satisfactorily analyzed."[42] The discords of the seventh may appear with or without their roots in all classes, whereas the only discord of the ninth that can appear in its complete form is that on the dominant.[43] The dominant seventh with the omitted root forms the triad on the leading tone. Goetschius had been reluctant to treat the leading-tone triad as an independent harmony; the dominant seventh provides a logical explanation both of the quality and of the function of this triad. The seventh-chord on the leading tone is similarly explained as a dominant ninth-chord with an omitted root.[44]

The single embarrassing moment in Goetschius's presentation of his theory of harmonic progression occurs in the exposition of the Second-class discords. He constructs a II7 chord with the root omitted and discovers that it is none other than the IV. "It is now theoretically apparent that the Triad II is the Principal representative of the 'Subdominant' harmony, while the IV is only an Incomplete form of the II7."[45] Goetschius further establishes the priority of the II by pointing out that it bears the same relation to the dominant that the dominant does to the tonic, namely, the descending harmonic degree.[46] His conclusion is an astonishing self-contradiction: "This confirms the theory that no chord-Root can be accepted upon any perfect fifth *below* the Keynote."[47] The subdominant triad, originally one of three principal triads of the key and one of the "three essential elements of harmony," is now seen not to exist independently at all, since "no chord-Root can be accepted upon any perfect fifth below the Keynote." This triad is now explained as being derived from a discord. On the other hand, the II, which was originally introduced as one of the subordinate triads, "interspersed occasionally for the sake of variety, contrast, and embellishment," has now risen to the rank of third-most important in Goetschius's system, after the tonic and the dominant.

The entire system of harmonic progression is shown in Figure 44. Goetschius explains it thus:

a. The chords in parenthesis are very rare.
b. The classes are a perfect fifth apart.
c. The Tonic Class is Inactive, the others are all Active.
d. The Normal (Regular) Progressions or Resolutions are made by each class one Grade from right to left (towards tonic).
e. The reversed progression (away from the Tonic) is the "Digression." This, and the progression of two Grades are both Irregular.
f. Every Regular progression is complete in itself, and entirely cancels the obligations of the Class. Every Irregular progression, on the contrary, is only a Partial Resolution, or none at all, and demands justification by subsequent Resolution. The best and commonest mode is, after every Irregular progression, to return immediately to the former Class.
g. The movements of the Triad III are eccentric.[48]

Goetschius's derivation of his theory of harmonic progression from its acoustic foundation bears examining. He uses the acoustically derived fifth as the fundamental unit of his theory, but with the important qualification that the natural movement by fifths is downward. Where does this qualification come from? What feature of the acoustically derived fifth suggests downward motion? If any natural movement seems suggested at all, it is upward, since an acoustical "root" produces primarily its own sound and only incidentally the sounds of its harmonics. The contention that the ear hears a "root" and

	Tonic Class	Dominant or First Class	Subdominant or Second Class		
Concords	I VI and Inversions	V (III) and Inversions	IV II and Inversions	3rd Class	4th Class
Discords		V7 V_0^7 V9 V_0^9 and inversions	II7 (II9) IV7 and inversions	VI7 VI9 I7	III7 III9 III in minor

Figure 44.   Table of the harmonic system of key (Goetschius,
Material Used, *p. 109)*

assumes an upper partial such as the fifth is at least defensible by the laws of physics. But Goetschius proposes the reverse, namely, that upon hearing a pitch the ear perceives it in the position of a harmonic and consequently demands a root a fifth below.

Such an objection can be answered simply. The success of Goetschius's theory depends entirely upon the satisfactory establishment of the tonic. Once the tonic has been clearly defined, other chord roots may be perceived as upper partials related to it. It is for this reason that the dominant is very useful in establishing a tonic; the sounding of the dominant suggests the note a fifth above itself, thereby demonstrating between the tonic and the second-dominant a relationship that would otherwise have been less obvious. The second-dominant note, then, demands its acoustical root, the dominant, which in turn demands *its* root, the tonic. Since the tonic has been established as the root of the entire structure the progression has no further obligations, but may move anywhere and begin again to be drawn back toward the tonic through the chain of fifths. Even in the "artificial" minor key this law of progression extends as far as the second-dominant.

The establishment of the tonic as the end of the

downward progression does not entirely clarify the concept of the subdominant. Goetschius relegates the subdominant to the Second class of chords, explaining that it is really an incomplete II7. This explanation suffices in a majority of instances, but not in such cases as the plagal cadence, in which the progression would be explained as skipping from the Second class past the First class to the tonic. Certainly there is nothing about the sound of the progression IV–I that might result from such a violent procedure as the elision of the dominant; on the contrary, the plagal cadence has traditionally been considered to produce a more restful and motionless effect than the unadorned authentic cadence.

Goetschius's difficulty with the subdominant should not eclipse the importance of his theory. Whereas European theorists had directed most of their efforts toward theories of chord construction, Goetschius presents an explanation of harmonic progression. The theory of natural movement of roots by fifths is not new; Rameau had proposed the same theory in Book II of the *Traité de l'harmonie*.[49] Subsequent European theorists had ignored this concept, however, in their excitement over Rameau's later theories. The theory of root progression by fifths might never have assumed its present importance in American theory had Goetschius not presented it. Moreover, he develops it by reducing the harmonies in a key to three principal classes, each class having its own defined obligations. Thus he presents an important principle of harmonic function.

The movement of chord roots by descending fifths is indeed perceived by the ear as a natural and logical harmonic motion; this theory is easily supported by musical practice. Moreover, Goetschius supplies his theory with an acoustic foundation that is at least credible; assuming the establishment of the tonic, each chord root is understood as the fifth of the next until the tonic itself is reached. Arthur Loesser recalls that Goetschius once exclaimed during a lecture on harmonic progression, "You see how those chords are drawn to the tonic center? It's like the law of gravitation; it *is* the law of gravitation!"[50] Goetschius's explanation of chord roots descending in fifths toward the tonic does indeed form a sort of theory of harmonic gravitation.

Altered and Mixed Chords; Modulation

Having defined the theory of tone-relations and its harmonic operation within a key, Goetschius must next explain the different effects produced by the appearance of tones foreign to the scale. Specifically, he must distinguish between casual chromatic alterations and tones which form modulations to new keys.

Goetschius defines altered chords as harmonies that contain one or more tones foreign to the scale but whose context shows them to be legitimate harmonies in the key. Tones foreign to the scale may be used in the key for melodic purposes, such as the confirmation or contradiction of the tendency of an active scale degree or the conversion of an inactive degree to active. Because the purpose of such a foreign tone is melodic, Goetschius warns that its use should not interfere with the legitimate harmonic progression. For this reason he limits the use of foreign tones to certain degrees of the scale, and these only in certain chords.[51]

Figure 45 shows the permissible altered scale degrees in a major key, according to Goetschius. The most common are *a*, the lowered sixth-scale degree in a First- or Second-class chord; *b*, the raised second in a First-class chord only; *c*, the raised fourth in a Second-class chord only; and *d*, the raised second and fourth degrees only in a Second-class chord.[52] It may be noted that, despite Goetschius's precaution, the joint use of the raised second and fourth degrees (shown at *d*) does interfere with the normal harmonic action by diverting the resolution of the Second-class chord from a First-class chord directly to a tonic chord. More rarely used are the raised first, fifth, and sixth

Figure 45.   Permissible altered scale-degrees in major keys

degrees, as shown at *e*, *f*, and *g*. These occur only in tonic or Third-class chords.[53]

Alterations in the minor scale are chiefly adjustments of the sixth and seventh scale degrees in order to remove the awkward augmented step. The sixth degree of the minor scale may be raised in First-, Second-, or Third-class chords, as shown in Figure 46*a*. The sixth usually progresses upward to the seventh degree, which is a member of a First-class chord. A descending seventh degree may be lowered (shown at *b*) in order to improve its tendency toward the sixth degree. This usually occurs in chords of the Third- or Fourth-classes. The lowered second degree (shown at *c*) is found in the II triad only, usually when the triad is in its first inversion. This accounts for the Neapolitan sixth-chord (not mentioned by this name) in minor. Goetschius does not acknowledge its use in major keys. The raised fourth degree may also be used in minor, as at *d*, but only in Second-class chords, and only in conjunction with the raised sixth degree. When a raised fourth degree is so employed, the accompanying raised sixth is relieved of its upward obligation and can progress either upward or downward.[54]

Figure 46. Permissible altered scale-degrees in minor keys

To indicate an altered note in a chord, Goetschius places an appropriate accidental above the Roman numeral in the chord symbol. The accidental usually does not refer specifically to the arabic numeral which it follows. The chord in the second measure of Figure 45*a*, for instance, is symbolized $\text{II}^{7\flat}$; the flat, however, refers not to the chord seventh, but to the sixth scale degree. The reader can determine this only by knowing that in a major key the only possible alteration by flattening is that of the sixth degree. Similarly, one may determine the altered members of the chord ^7II ♯♯ only by knowing that the only double alteration in a Second-class chord is that of the second and fourth degrees. This system is made more complicated by the few cases in which the arabic numeral does refer to the accidental. The altered chord in Figure 45*e*, for instance, is symbolized $^5_1$♯ , showing the raised fifth. The arabic 5 is used to distinguish it from the chord in Figure 45*f*, symbolized $^♯_1$ (altered root).

Goetschius says that the distinctive feature of the "mixed" chords is the interval of the augmented sixth. Because of the augmented sixth, these chords do not have the shape of ordinary triads or discords and are therefore irregular, or "deformed."[55] In major keys, mixed First- or Second-class chords are possible, as shown in Figure 47*a* and *b*; the only mixed chords available in minor keys are those of the Second class, shown at *c*. The Second-class mixed chords are the Italian, French, and German sixth-chords (Goetschius does not use these names). Goetschius prefers that the German sixth-chord in major be spelled with the raised second-degree rather than the lowered third, which he considers erroneous: "This common error is probably owing to an instinctive reluctance to associating D-sharp with A-flat when E-flat appears to be so much more plausible and natural; or it may also be owing to a thoughtless confusion of the Major and Minor Modes. C major cannot have an E-flat, as that is the very tone which distinguishes it from C minor."[56] The symbols for mixed chords, shown in Figure 47, are similar to those for altered chords.

Figure 47.   Mixed chords

It should be noted that Goetschius makes a distinction between foreign tones used in altered chords and tones which are actually members of another key:

When the chord which follows (and, as is probable, the chord which precedes, also) confirms the original Key, then no change of Key takes place, and the foreign tone is merely a casual chromatic inflection of the corresponding scale tone. In this case [Figure 48a]: the accidental is not an actual F-sharp, in its legitimate personality as leading tone of G major, but merely "F-raised" or "F-altered"—not "F-sharp" in the ordinary sense. But if, on the contrary, the next chord corroborates the foreign tone, as Tonic Chord of the Key which that tone seems to represent, thus [Figure 48b]: then it proves to be an actual F-sharp in its genuine capacity as Leading-tone of G major.[57]

Figure 48.   Goethschius, Material Used, *p. 124*

Goetschius's distinction between F-raised and F-sharp in this case is a rather fine one. It becomes even more difficult when he states that the altered tone is " 'borrowed' from a related scale."[58] (The "borrowed-note" explanation, which Faisst had also used,[59] appears to be the source of the appellation "mixed chord," since the chord borrows tones from two foreign keys.) Moreover, Goetschius states that altered chords "represent the most fugitive grade of Key-association, or, more strictly, are only *incipient* modulations, not consummated by regular resolution into the Key to which they legitimately belong, according to their notation."[60] According to Goetschius, then, Figure 49a contains an "incipient" modulation toward G major, which is thwarted by the tonic chord following the chord at the asterisk. The passage remains in C major throughout. The F-sharp, though borrowed from the related scale of G, is really only the altered fourth scale degree of C major. Figure 49b shows a genuine modulation to G major before the cadence in C.

Figure 49 shows that Goetschius identifies a modulation in the same manner that Prout does, namely, by the single chord following the accidental: "If the following Chord confirms the Key suggested by the foreign tone, then these two chords together constitute a more or less complete Modulation, or change of Key."[61] Yet the difference in the effect of Figure 49 at *a*

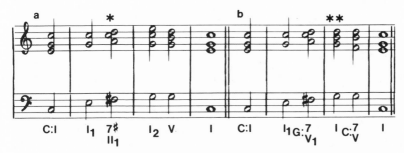

Figure 49. Goetschius's distinction between an altered chord and modulation

and *b* is a small one. Goetschius defines a modulation as "the process by which a transition is made from one Key or Mode to another."[62] According to his reasoning, the tonality of the example in Figure 49*b* shifts from C major to G major and back. That is, C relinquishes its position as the tonal center to which all harmony is drawn, and this position is taken over by G. The key of G does indeed draw the D discord to itself. But when the triad on G is reached, the sense of accomplishment and repose that is characteristic of a tonic, according to Goetschius, is not present. Few listeners would admit that the chord marked with two asterisks has the finality of a tonic triad; rather, the effect is that of a dominant in C major. In this case, then, no audible transition from C major to G major has been made, although the necessary mechanics of modulation appear to be present.

In order to deal with short "modulations" in which the new tonality immediately yields to the old one, Goetschius distinguishes between transient and complete modulations. "A Modulation is distinguished as *complete*, when the prospective key becomes the final aim of the digression, and is confirmed as such by a complete Perfect Cadence in the new Scale."[63] Such modulations are large in scope and are represented by a complete phrase, or at least a substantial portion of the phrase. A transient modulation is a much more localized event: "A modulation is distinguished as *transient*, when the new Key occurs in the course of a Phrase or Period, and is followed either by the original Key again, or by some other next-related Key. Transient modulations are frequently very brief, only extending through a few beats, sometimes only including two chords, but not less than two."[64] Since a new key is usually entered through its dominant,[65] the simplest transient modulation is formed by any major or minor triad preceded by its dominant chord. The purpose of a transient modulation, according to Goetschius, is to emphasize an important major or minor triad by presenting it as the tonic of a new key: "Every Major or Minor Triad which occupied an accented beat, may become a Tonic Triad (of the corresponding Key, of course), provided that the preceding Melody-note can be harmonized with any Dominant Chord of that Key."[66] Figure 50 shows a progression in which transient modulations are used to intensify the triads marked with asterisks.

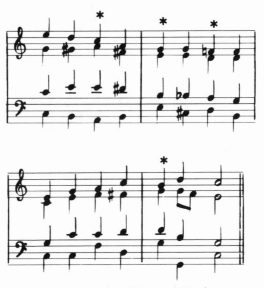

Figure 50. Goetschius, Material Used, *p. 181*

After Goetschius has convincingly stated that a tonic is the final goal and resolution of the obligations of chord progression in a key, it is somewhat surprising that he accepts such chords as those marked with asterisks in Figure 50 as tonic harmonies—even transient tonics. Each of these chords admittedly fulfills the obligation of the dominant chord that precedes it; this is intentional, otherwise the dominant chord would not be so placed at all. However, the single dominant preceding the "tonic" chord marked with an asterisk is not sufficient to establish it as a new key center.

The problem of analyzing such localized modulations is not new; the German and English theorists had also regarded them as transient modulations. Weber had remarked that such small "modulations" are so transient that they scarcely deserve the name. By following the practice of the European theorists and distinguishing between "complete" and "transient" modulations, Goetschius at least shows that he is aware of the lack of modulatory effect of the latter. Nonetheless, to regard such a brief event as a "modulation"—a replacement of a previous tonal center with a new one—remains something of an abuse of Goetschius's own concept of the tonic. Transient modulation would become the subject of debate among subsequent American theorists.

Goetschius succeeds in establishing a convincing definition of nearly related keys. He admits as nearest relatives of any key the keys of its dominant, subdominant, and relative minor, and the dominant and subdominant of the relative minor. The nearly related keys to C major are F and G major and A, D, and E minor. Goetschius's results, then, are much like those of Prout's. However, in explaining these key relationships Goetschius has a notable advantage in his acknowledgment of the theoretical significance of the Aeolian form of the minor scale.[67] He states that the relationships between keys are determined "firstly and chiefly, according to the number of tones which the Scales possess in common; and secondly, according to certain important coincidences, or points of contact (of single tones or Chords)."[68] The relative minor key may be admitted because it has, in its Aeolian form, precisely the same notes as its original major key. The dominant and subdominant keys of the relative minor, in their Aeolian forms, each differ by only one note from the original major key and may therefore also be admitted.

Besides the comparison of scales, Goetschius gives the device shown in Figure 51 which may be used to discover nearly related keys. Each triad of the original key may represent the tonic triad of a nearly related key (except the diminished triad, which of course cannot be a tonic). If the original key is minor, the triads are reckoned from the notes of the descending melodic form of the scale, which coincides with the Aeolian form.[69] This method is useful not only for finding nearly related keys but also

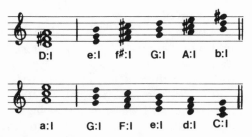

Figure 51. Goetschius, Material Used, p. 139

as a demonstration of harmonic points of contact between a key and its nearest relatives.

According to Goetschius, any key has not only its five most nearly related keys but also has several remotely related keys. A minor key is remotely related to its dominant major key, or, conversely, a major key is remotely related to its minor subdominant. For this relationship Goetschius adopts the colorful term the "Stride." "This relationship, although 'Remote,' because there is a difference of four Accidentals in the signature, is quite as intimate as any Next-related Key, and the modulation from one Key to another is as easy and natural as if they were actually next-related."[70] The basis of the "Stride" relationship is the harmonic degree, the fifth, which lies between the two tonics. The practical connection is the coincidence of the tonic triad of a major key with the dominant triad (with raised leading tone) of a minor key.[71]

Another important distant relationship between keys is formed when the tonic note of a key coincides with the mediant of another, such as C major and A-flat major, or C major and E major. This relationship is sometimes found between two keys that are already nearly related, such as C major and A minor.[72]

Goetschius classifies the opposite mode of a key as one of its distant relatives. The key of C minor, which Goetschius had discovered to be an "artificial" alteration of C major, and whose tonic note is the same as that of C major, is related to it only distantly because of a difference of three notes.[73] In the final cadence in Figure 52, then, there is a modulation from C minor to its distantly related key of C major. Goetschius's definition of modulation allows "a change from one Key or Mode into another," according to which the change of a mode is a genuine

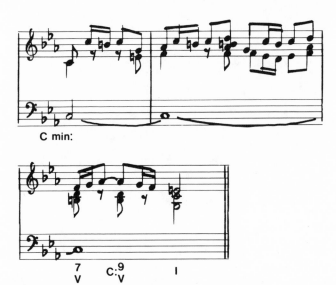

Figure 52. *Bach, "Fugue in C minor" from* Das Whohltemperiere Clavier

modulation. The designation of it as a modulation to a distantly related key is misleading, however; although the constituencies of the two scales include two or three uncommon notes, the two tonic centers are not separated by any harmonic degrees.

Goetschius distinguishes between diatonic and chromatic modulation. A diatonic modulation uses a chord common to both keys directly before the introduction of the new accidental; the harmonic action to and from this common chord is regulated by the law of diatonic chord progression in one key or the other. In Figure 53(a) the A minor chord is approached as the submediant of C major, then progresses as the second dominant of G major. In a chromatic modulation there is no such common chord; rather, the new accidental is introduced directly by a chromatic change, such as the F-F-sharp in the bass in Figure 52(b). Goetschius states that chromatic modulations "are more abrupt and striking, and consequently more effective, than Diatonic transitions."[74]

Goetschius's use of the term "chromatic" conforms strictly to the definition proposed by Nicolà Vincentino, involving the "large" semitone (F-F-sharp, as opposed to the diatonic F-G-flat). Goetschius regards chromatic changes as

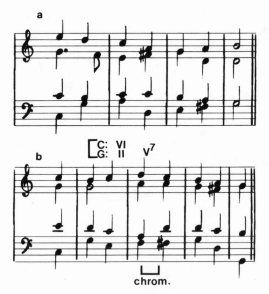

Figure 53.   Goetschius, Material Used, p. 143

unnatural because of the huge distance in harmonic degrees
separating such notes: "The result of such an inflection is much
greater than it appears to be, and can only be correctly
appreciated by comparing the two tones as Key-notes,
which . . . indicates their actual distance apart in harmonic
degrees. This test proves that every chromatic progression is
actually a leap of *seven degrees*."[75] The logic of such progressions is
evident not from the natural scale but only by apparent
proximity; "The change (for which there can hardly be any
theoretical justification) must be accounted for and excused on
purely practical grounds, namely: the *apparent* distance (i.e., to the
ear) is so short, being but a half-step, that the ear, far from
experiencing any difficulty, rather evinces an inclination to
follow and apprehend the progression."[76]

    Goetschius's theory of natural harmonic progression,
then, does not extend to chromatic movement:

To the Chromatic domain pertain all connections between any two
chords which belong peculiarly to different keys. Here, no natural law
of chord succession can be laid down and defended, because the chord-
relations cannot be defined from a common centre; any imaginable

succession is possible, and it is difficult even to systematize, in some degree, the almost inexhaustible multitude of possibilities in this domain. "Chromatics" is the domain of harmonic Lawlessness. While the chord-associations in the diatonic sphere are the unconstrained consequence of natural conditions, the chord-associations in the chromatic sphere are a direct violation of these natural conditions, and are effected by artificial means (i.e. by means of the apparently delicate, but in reality most powerful, chromatic "lever," which inflects the chord in such a way as to destroy its contact with its Tonic and cancel its obligations to the latter).[77]

The regard of chromatic progressions as the "domain of harmonic Lawlessness" is attributed by Mother Carroll to Goetschius's personal aversion to the chromatic harmony that was being used by late Romantic composers. In this regard she observes: "Goetschius was intransigent in his loyalty to the tonal system exploited by his favorite composers of the nineteenth century, and he regarded with disfavor the innovations of Wagner, Strauss, Debussy, et al."[78] Both *The Material Used in Musical Composition* and *The Theory and Practice of Tone-Relations* (especially the earlier editions) contain admonitions to harmony students to avoid using as models the "adventurous explorers" of the late nineteenth century.[79] Even so, he could have formulated some system to account for chromatic progressions had he not already acknowledged his pattern of fifth-relations as the "natural" system. As he himself points out, the interval of a chromatic semitone between two tones is actually a distance of seven harmonic degrees. He has no choice, then, but to regard the proximity of two such tones as artificial. Moreover, he states that chromatic alterations do not affect the natural harmonic progression. When a chromatic inflection does deflect its chord from the normal resolution, the progression must simply be considered beyond the bounds of his system.

Nonharmonic Tones

It has been noted that Goetschius admits only chords of the seventh and ninth as harmonic discords. Eleventh- and thirteenth-"chords" are not recognized as legitimate harmonies at all, since the proportion of dissonances to consonances is extremely high in such combinations (see Figure 54a). He also rejects as chords any groups of simultaneous tones organized by intervals other than thirds, such as those in Figure 54*b*.[80] In short, any combination not readily apparent as either a triad or a seventh- or ninth-chord is not recognized as a pure harmony, but as one containing nonharmonic tones. "It is true that dissonances are often multiplied, so that occasionally even all seven letters of the scale are associated simultaneously—for example, at * [see Figure 55]. But such dissonances are never 'chords!' "[81] Combinations such as the one in Figure 55, which Prout would have identified as a second-inversion supertonic major thirteenth-chord, are analyzed by Goetschius as clusters predominantly of nonharmonic tones.

Figure 54.   *Goetschius,* Tone-Relations, *p. 135*

Figure 55.   *Mendelssohn, Op. 82 (Goetschius,* Tone-Relations, *p. 12)*

Goetschius, like the European theorists, classifies nonharmonic tones according to the manner in which they are approached and resolved: "There are four kinds of Inharmonic tones: the Organ-point, the Suspension, the Anticipation, and the Neighboring-Note; which are distinguished according to the manner in which they enter and progress."[82] His classifications become encumbered, however, with descriptions of exceptional and irregular entrances and progressions of these tones. Thus, his alternate distinction is useful: "They may also be divided into three groups, as follows: The Organ-point is a *heavy* (long) embellishment, the Neighboring-Note is a *light* (short) embellishment, and the Suspension and Anticipation result from partial *mixture* of a chord with those which precede or follow it."[83] The implications of the terms "heavy," "light," and "chord-mixture" in this case seem to go beyond designating mere duration or prominence; they indicate the degree of urgency of resolution. The organ-point is described as a "heavy, impassive tone, which effects its 'Resolution' by simply remaining until the other intervals return to mutual consonance."[84] The "light" tones and those resulting from mixtures of chord elements are more active and demand resolution more urgently.

Goetschius's exposition of the organ-point is excellent. The purpose of organ-point, he says, is "to strengthen the impression of some important tone of the Scale by prolongation."[85] Because the tonic and the dominant are usually the only tones of sufficient importance to deserve such emphasis, they produce the most successful organ-points. He observes that the tonic and the dominant organ-points are actually realizations of the two tones, which the listener is mentally retaining anyway:

> The prolongation of the Tonic or Dominant notes as Organ-points is justifiable on the grounds that these are naturally the most prevalent, dominating tones of the Key, and whether they are merely retained in the mind as ideal prolongations of those factors from which all the relations of the Key must be determined, or are actually held and kept sounding in the ear, is not a matter of great difference; in fact, the latter seems the most natural course to pursue.[86]

According to Goetschius the organ-point may appear in the bass or in any of the upper parts. It must begin and end as a harmonic tone. It may be sustained or reiterated. An organ-point becomes incorrect when the harmonies above it modulate to a remote key or become too harshly discordant with it, as in Figure 56.

Figure 56. Goetschius, Material Used, *p. 187*

The tonic and the dominant may be sustained together in the bass as a double organ-point. He names this effect the "Pastoral Organ-point."[87]

Irregular organ-points sustain degrees other than the tonic or dominant. Of these he considers the mediant the best, because of its inactive status and its membership in the tonic triad.[88] Other degrees are used only rarely as organ-points. He calls attention to the "short Organ-point" which extends through only three chords and is nonharmonic to the second of them (an example of a "short Organ-point" is given in Figure 57). These are generally used to avoid inconvenient movement of one of the voices. The effect is still "heavy" because of the passive manner of resolution.

Figure 57.   Goetschius, Material Used, p. 193

Goetschius's initial rules for the use of the suspension are traditional. The suspension must be a tone that is a member of the first of two chords; must be sustained into the second chord, of which it is not a member; and must be resolved by step, usually downward. A suspension must occur on a strong fraction of a beat, preferably on a strong beat of the measure, and should remain suspended for at least half the value of the chord before resolving.[89]

Having given rules for the use of the suspension, Goetschius proceeds to make a series of exceptions. The first of these regards the "harmonic suspension."

It is not absolutely necessary that the tone which is prolonged in this manner from one Chord over into the next, should become an Inharmonic dissonance. . . . Very often the prolonged note agrees with the Intervals of the following Chord, so that they together assume the appearance, at least, of a Harmonic body. When this is the case the prolonged note is called a "Harmonic" Suspension; and it will nevertheless produce the effect of an ordinary Inharmonic Suspension, if the apparent "Chord" does not conform to the harmonic progression which is expected or required.[90]

In Figure 58(*a*), the chord progression is V7–I, the natural progression, rather than the unlikely V7–III–I. Since III is not expected to follow V7, the second chord is perceived as I with a suspended B, which resolves upward to the chord tone C. The root and third of a precadential second-inversion tonic chord form a pair of just such harmonic suspensions, provided that they have been prepared, as at *b*. In fact, according to Goetschius, an entire chord may be suspended into an accented position, deferring the expected chord to a weak fraction of the beat, as shown in Figure 59.

Figure 58. Harmonic suspensions (*Goetschius,* Material Used, *p. 198)*

Figure 59. *Goetschius,* Material Used, *p. 198*

This is certainly not a traditional description of a suspension. Goetschius deserves credit for recognizing that the "harmonic suspension" has an effect similar to that of an orthodox suspension, especially in regard to rhythm and expected chord progression. Nevertheless, to classify it as a suspension is at least questionable. Goetschius himself has stated that suspensions are formed by the mixing of elements of two chords. In the "harmonic suspension" the second of the two chords is stated only partially or not at all; its complete form is only implied by the law of natural progression. Moreover, the traditionally recognized motivating element of a suspension is dissonance. It is this dissonance which impels the suspension to its resolution. In a "harmonic suspension" such as those shown in Figures 58 and 59, the element of dissonance is lacking, and the obligation to resolution is accordingly weakened. The concept of such a "harmonic nonharmonic tone" must thus be regarded as something of a contradiction.

The licenses which Goetschius permits in the preparation of a suspension are unusual. He states that it is not necessary for a suspension to appear in the same voice that prepares it: "A tone which appears in a lower part may re-appear in the following chord as Suspension in the Soprano, entering with a skip, or diatonically, as the case may be. Or the Suspension may represent an interval which does not actually appear in the preceding chord, but is understood as possible Seventh, or (if sufficiently plausible) as possible Ninth of the latter."[91] The D in Figure 60(*a*) is prepared in the alto voice, then suspended in the soprano. At *b* the suspended note E is "prepared" by being understood as a seventh of the IV. Goetschius does not point out that these "suspensions" also fit the definitions he is about to give of the appoggiatura and the accented passing tone.

Figure 60. *Irregular preparation of the suspension (Goetschius,* Material Used, *p. 204)*

The exceptions to the rules for the anticipation mirror those regarding the suspension. An anticipation may be dissonant to the harmony during which it sounds, or it may be harmonic, as in the example in Figure 61.[92] Since the anticipation is not compelled to move to resolve, the lack of dissonance in a "harmonic anticipation" is perhaps a bit more plausible than its analogous suspension. Nonetheless, the dissonance of an anticipation leads the ear to expect the remainder of the chord to follow.

6   5

Figure 61.   Harmonic anticipation (Goetschius, Material Used, p. 209)

Goetschius explains that the anticipation may be resolved irregularly just as the suspension is prepared irregularly. That is, the anticipation may progress by skipping, while the note it anticipates appears in another voice, as at the asterisk in Figure 62; or it is understood as a seventh or ninth of the next chord, as at the double asterisk. Thus Goetschius derives the escape tone from the anticipation, as Prout does.[93]

Figure 62.   Goetschius, Material Used, p. 215

Goetschius permits the anticipation to prepare the suspension, as in Figure 63.[94] This procedure violates the purpose of both nonharmonic tones; the anticipation does not "anticipate" the following harmony, nor does the suspension prolong an element of the preceding chord. This use of the anticipation and suspension is in direct contradiction to Goetschius's concept of chord mixture, since the nonharmonic element is a member of neither chord. Such a nonharmonic tone might be better described as some sort of passing tone.

Figure 63. Goetschius, Material Used, p. 212

Goetschius classifies neighboring notes as either "local" or "progressive" embellishments. The "local" neighboring note is used to embellish only a single chord tone. Upper neighboring notes are spelled according to the scale; lower neighboring notes lie a semitone beneath the chord tone, except that the lower neighbor of the leading tone is diatonic.[95] The "progressive" neighboring note is the passing tone. It may be either accented or unaccented, and it may proceed diatonically or chromatically. Chromatic passing tones generally ascend; used descending they sound "peculiar, and often ridiculously lugubrious."[96] Goetschius recommends that in a passage containing both diatonic and chromatic passing tones the larger intervals be used first, as in Figure 64(a). Chromatic passing tones must be spelled according to the rules for altered scale degrees; the passing tone in Figure 64b must be spelled F-sharp, because G-flat is too foreign to the key of C.[97]

Figure 64. Chromatic passing tones (Goetschius, Material Used, p. 219)

As in the case of the other nonharmonic tones, Goetschius admits an irregular use of the neighboring note: "Either the upper or lower Neighboring-note may be placed before its principal tone, without regard to what precedes (i.e., irrespective of the manner in which they are introduced— whether with a skip, or after a Rest, or at the very beginning of the Phrase, or in the strict diatonic manner shown in the former lessons)."[98] When approached by a skip, the note is called an appoggiatura.[99] Goetschius deviates from tradition by permitting the use of the appoggiatura on unaccented as well as accented fractions of the beat.

It is unfortunate that Goetschius is unable or unwilling to develop his classifications "light," "heavy," and "mixture" in his treatment of nonharmonic tones. If he had, he would have left subsequent American theorists a very useful system by which to consider these tones. As it is, he follows the established practice of classifying nonharmonic tones according to the manner in which they are approached and resolved. In doing so, he admits a series of licenses and irregularities which renders the entire system unwieldy. Some of his nonharmonic tones fit two categories (e.g., the irregularly prepared suspension, which is also an irregularly prepared neighboring note); others, such as the harmonic suspension, are not really nonharmonic tones at all. Subsequent American theorists would be obliged to disregard many of Goetschius's exceptions in their organization of nonharmonic tones.

3

An Age of Synthesis: 1897–1939

American Harmony Texts, 1897–1905: George Chadwick, Arthur Foote and Walter Spalding, Francis York, Benjamin Cutter

In his 1922 textbook, *Harmony for Ear, Eye, and Keyboard*, Arthur E. Heacox includes an appendix of books to be used for reference and further reading. Under the heading "A Few of the Widely Used Standard Texts," Heacox lists Goetschius's *Theory and Practice of Tone-Relations*, as well as the treatises of Prout, Richter, and Solomon Jadassohn. Heacox also includes in his list George Chadwick's *Harmony* (1897), Francis York's *Harmony Simplified* (1897–1900), and *Modern Harmony in its Theory and Practice* (1905) by Arthur Foote and Walter Spalding. Benjamin Cutter's *Harmonic Analysis* (1902) is also listed, as a "specialty" book.[1]

Heacox's list is a good representation of the theories that were being read by American harmony students during the first quarter of the twentieth century. Goetschius's theory, to be sure, had achieved recognition through his books as well as his activity as a teacher, but it had by no means displaced Richter's system. Richter's *Lehrbuch* had been popular in the United States since its first American translation in 1867. In 1884 the *Lehrbuch der Harmonie* of Solomon Jadassohn, Richter's successor at Leipzig, made its first appearance in translation in the United States.[2] Jadassohn's work hardly differs from that of Richter.

The influence of Richter and Jadassohn was felt not only through their own works but also through the writings of their American students. The most popular of these volumes before 1890 was *Elements of Harmony* (1879) by Stephen A. Emery, a student of Richter who later taught at the New England Conservatory. Emery's book bears a close resemblance in most respects to Richter's. The composer George W. Chadwick and the pianist Frank H. Shepard (*Harmony Simplified*, 1896) both studied in Leipzig before returning to the United States and writing works on harmony. Benjamin Cutter studied at the New England Conservatory with Stephen Emery. Arthur Foote and Walter Spalding were familiar with Richter's *Lehrbuch* from their studies with John Knowles Paine.

Harmony books by American authors between 1897 and 1905 reveal a gradual absorption of several features of Goetschius's theory into a field of thought dominated by Richter. Some theorists, notably Francis York and Benjamin Cutter, made use of Goetschius's ideas surprisingly early in the period. Other authors—including Thomas Tapper (*First Year Harmony*, 1908) and Howard Elmore Parkhurst (*Harmony*, 1908)—adhered strictly to Richter's system even after Goetschius's ideas had made an impact on American theoretical thought. In general, however, it may be said that during the period around 1900 certain features of Richter's theory would assume permanent places in American theoretical practice, while the ideas of Goetschius (and, to a lesser extent, Prout) would begin to intermingle with them.

The most apparent feature to be adapted by American writers from Richter's theory is the system of chord symbols. Of course, the representation of chord roots by Roman numerals had already become a standard practice. However, although Goetschius had used only uppercase Roman numerals, Richter's system of uppercase and lowercase numerals and the signs ° and either ' or + to indicate major, minor, diminished and augmented chords found its way into the works of American writers. Frank Shepard uses the system exactly as Richter had, even retaining Richter's original apostophe ' (instead of the symbol +, which was replacing it in American publications) to indicate the augmented chord.[3] Shepard uses figured-bass numerals independently of the chord symbols to show inversions, as Richter had.

George Chadwick, in *Harmony*, uses the system of uppercase and lowercase numerals and the sign°.[4] Chadwick appears to be the first American author to combine figured-bass characters with Roman numerals, giving an "absolute" system of figuring in which both the chord root and the inversion are shown in a single symbol (e.g., ii^6_5; I^6_4).

Richter's symbols are also found in the works of Francis York, Benjamin Cutter, and Arthur Foote and Walter Spalding. To show inversions of chords, York uses a system involving the letters a, b, c, and d in subscript. A chord whose root is in the bass is said to be in the "a" position; the first and second inversions are the "b" and "c" positions, respectively.[5] Figure 65 shows the application of the system. The system of subscript letters seems to have been popular around 1900. Benjamin Cutter appends to the Roman numerals either subscript letters or figured-bass characters (he seems to prefer the latter).[6] Although the system is reminiscent of Goetschius's subscript numerals, it may have had a European origin; it is used by Ebenezer Prout in the sixteenth edition of his treatise.[7]

la   lb   lc

Figure 65.   Inversions indicated by subscript letters

Another reflection of Richter's theory in American harmony works is the designation of the tonic, dominant, and subdominant triads as principal triads because of their connection with the scale and the key. This concept, which had been borrowed from Rameau by Weber and transported to the United States by Richter's Lehrbuch, appears in modified form in nearly every harmony book of the time. It should be noted that, unlike Richter, the American theorists do not actually construct the scale from the three principal triads, but only observe that every note of the scale is contained in these three chords. Shepard states that the principal triads are so designated because: "(a.) They are the most frequently used. (b.) They embrace every note of the scale. (c.) They are sufficient to determine, beyond a doubt, the key."[8] Chadwick uses the principal triads for a pedagogical purpose: "As these triads contain every note of the scale, it is evident that a melody that is strictly diatonic may be harmonized with these chords alone, provided that they can be made to progress legitimately from one to another."[9] The modification by which the principal triads only reflect the scale, rather than act as its source, may be traced to Jadassohn, who also gives such an explanation in his *Lehrbuch*.[10]

Richter had considered the secondary triads to include not only ii, iii, and vi, but also vii°. The inclusion of vii° among the secondary triads occurs in the works of Shepard, Chadwick, Foote and Spalding, Tapper, and Parkhurst.[11] Had these writers followed Goetschius's system, they would not have considered vii° to be an independent triad at all. Shepard and Parkhurst also retain Richter's classification of the seventh-chords, according to which the dominant seventh-chord is the only "primary" chord of the seventh, while the others are all "secondary."[12]

Whereas Goetschius had permitted only certain scale degrees to be altered chromatically, Richter had formed altered chords by raising or lowering any of the scale degrees. Most American theorists around 1900 seem to prefer Richter's method. Benjamin Cutter, for example, writes "any step of a scale, major or minor, may be changed chromatically."[13] Chadwick also permits any scale degree to be altered chromatically: "When the progression of any voice by one whole step is subdivided into two half steps by the chromatic expansion or contraction of the interval, tones are introduced which are foreign to the key."[14] Foote and Spalding agree: "Theoretically, any factor of a triad or of a seventh- or of a ninth-chord may be chromatically raised or lowered."[15]

Richter's terminology appears in some American writers' explanation of nonharmonic tones. The term "by-tone," which Richter had used to refer to a harmonic tone in a series of passing tones (see p. 18, Figure 13) is found in York's work with a different meaning. According to York, a by-tone is a chord member appearing only after the chord is sounded, as at the asterisk in Figure 66.[16] In a later work, *Applied Harmony* (1917), by

Figure 66. A by-tone (York, p. 60)

Carolyn Alchin, the term "by-tone" is used as a synonym for "non-harmonic tone."[17] Foote and Spalding mention "passing chords" but do not discuss them in detail.[18]

The passing-chord concept appears in a curious circumstance in Shepard's explanation of second-inversion triads. Shepard permits second-inversion chords to be used in connection with chords on the same bass (as in Figure 67a), with chords of the same root (as at b), and with chords on neighboring bass tones (as at c). As a fourth category, Shepard presents the second-inversion chord used as a passing-chord, as shown at d.[19] Shepard's distinction between the uses shown at c and at d apparently results from a careless combination of Richter's and Goetschius's rules for the use of the second inversion.

Figure 67.   The uses of the second-inversion triad (Shepard, p. 205)

The European influence on American theorists around 1900 includes a few elements of the work of Ebenezer Prout. Shepard gives a brief demonstration of the harmonic series, referring to it as "Nature's Chord." He states that the major triad and the chords of the dominant seventh and ninth are modeled after the harmonic series: "A chord, as commonly understood, is an imitation, at the hands of Man, of the great chord of Nature, or at least it has been made to correspond very closely with it."[20] George Chadwick, decidedly not an adherent of Prout's theory, is at least familiar with the British terminology. Chadwick uses the term "generator" to refer to the dominant as the real root of the leading-tone seventh-chord.[21] He also uses the term "changing-tone," as does Prout, to refer to an anticipation that resolves by leap.[22] Francis York includes in his work a brief exposition of chords of the eleventh and thirteenth.[23]

Prout's influence is most pronounced in *Modern Harmony in its Theory and Practice*, by Arthur Foote and Walter Spalding. Spalding, not Foote, was responsible for the British elements in *Modern Harmony*. After studying with Paine, Spalding had travelled to Paris and Munich for further musical education before being appointed to teach at Harvard in 1895. At some point Spalding had become quite familiar with Prout's work. Spalding's *Tonal Counterpoint* (1904) is very much indebted to Prout's volume on the same subject, and in a few instances Spalding refers the reader to Prout for information on harmony and form.[24]

In *Modern Harmony* the authors refer several times to Prout's work *Harmony*. They quote Prout's statements regarding nearly related keys and the introduction of nondominant seventh-chords. Their practical demonstration of consonant and dissonant intervals and chords is a remarkably close paraphrase of a similar exposition in Prout's work.[25]

It should be noted that Foote and Spalding do not adopt Prout's acoustical theory of the three natural discords. It is possible that they refer to the 1901 revision of Prout's treatise, which had been in print in the United States for four years. In any case they do present an abbreviated exposition of chords of the eleventh and thirteenth, with the qualification that the higher dissonances are usually only nonharmonic tones. The authors state that seventh- and ninth-chords are considered independent harmonies only because they are frequently introduced without preparation of the dissonance; only if an eleventh or thirteenth is introduced without such preparation may the chord be considered a true independent eleventh- or thirteenth-chord.[26] The authors' examples include not only the famous thirteenth-chord from the beginning of the last movement of Beethoven's Ninth Symphony, but also an illustration of a true independent thirteenth-chord (with omitted third and fifth) from Debussy's *Pelléas and Mélisande* (Figure 68).

Figure 68.   Debussy, **Pelléas and Mélisande** *(Foote and Spalding, p. 169)*

Prout's recommended spelling of the chromatic scale is given by Foote and Spalding as its "grammatically correct spelling."[27] It will be recalled that Prout had spelled the chromatic scale of C using flats, rather than sharps, except for the raised fourth-scale degree, because these were the accidentals he had discovered in his three natural discords.[28] When this spelling is used independently of its basis, as in *Modern Harmony*, it appears rather foolish. Fortunately, the authors themselves do not take seriously this spelling of the chromatic scale in their exposition of altered chords. Had they done so, for instance, the dominant triad with the raised fifth would be spelled as an inverted mediant triad with a lowered root, as in Figure 69*b*. (Foote and Spalding spell it as in *a*.) Similar disfigurations would occur in other altered chords involving raised degrees other than the fourth.

Figure 69.   Foote and Spalding, p. 117

Foote and Spalding make several statements contradicting elements of Goetschius's theory. In their discussion of the scale degrees, they state: "The seventh tone of the scale, always a semitone below the tonic, is of especial importance, since it is the only one that has of itself a distinct tendency to move in a particular direction."[29] By elimination, then, the second, fourth, and sixth degrees have no such tendencies. Foote and Spalding also disagree with the order of importance and frequency that Goetschius had assigned the secondary triads. Whereas Goetschius had considered the ii more closely associated with the key, and consequently more frequently used, Foote and Spalding observe that: "triads I, IV, V, and vi are the ones most used, ii and iii less often."[30]

The authors' most sensible disagreements with Goetschius's theory are those involving the nonharmonic tones. In their exposition of the neighboring tone (for which they use Prout's term "auxiliary"), they dispense with rules specifying whether upper or lower auxiliaries should neighbor the principal note by a whole tone or a semitone.[31] They require the suspension to form a dissonance: "As the dissonant element is of prime importance, a really good suspension should form a dissonance of a seventh, a second, or a ninth with some one of the integral tones of the chord."[32] They also insist that the suspension be prepared in the voice that ultimately sounds it: "If we write a.) [Figure 70] instead of b.), we have no suspension at all, but an appoggiatura."[33]

Figure 70.   Foote and Spalding, p. 200

The most important elements of Goetschius's theory to be absorbed into the works of American theorists around 1900 is the concept of natural chord progression by root movements of descending fifths. It should be remembered that neither Richter's nor Prout's theories included any provision governing natural chord progression. Goetschius's theory of natural progression therefore had filled a significant void in theoretical knowledge, and American theorists of the turn of the century were quick to recognize it. The theory of root movements by descending fifths appears in the works of Francis York, George Chadwick, and Benjamin Cutter. Frank Shepard states that the natural progression of chord roots is by ascending fourths—possibly an adaptation of Goetschius's theory intended to appear original.[34]

The theory of natural root progression by fifths plays an important part in the work of Francis York. It is a tribute to Goetschius's work that, only six years after its American publication, it could influence a writer as remote from the Eastern cultural community as York. A native of extreme upper Michigan, York studied piano in Detroit and Boston (before 1889) and in Paris. He returned to Michigan to teach music at the State Normal College in Ypsilanti, and later headed the Detroit Conservatory. York's *Harmony Simplified* first appeared as a series of magazine articles in 1895; these were collected and published as a book in 1897.[35]

The theory of root movement by fifths appears at the outset of York's system: "Each chord, except I, has a more or less strong tendency to move to some special one of the other chords —usually to that chord whose root is five tones lower."[36] York refers to this principle throughout the work. He states that the "normal" progression of ii is to V, that of vi is to ii, and that of iii is to vi.[37] His explanation of the weakness of the mediant triad is an echo of Goetschius: "By remoteness from the I is meant that if we follow the normal progression of the chords, it will take four progressions to reach the I. Thus: iii, vi, ii, V, I. The relationship between the mediant and the I is not readily grasped, and so the chord is not much used."[38]

York attempts to reconcile the subdominant triad with the natural progression of fifths by citing the tonic as the goal of all harmonic progression: "As all chords have a tendency towards the I, the IV goes to the I either directly or first to the V, and then to the I."[39] York thus admits two exceptions to the theory of root progression by descending fifths. First, the root movement of the progression IV–I is that of an ascending fifth. Second, York does not present the progression IV–V as a form of ii–V. He thus admits into his system one common progression, IV–V, whose root movement does not even adhere to the normal interval.

York borrows Goetschius's system of triad classification. According to York, the triads I, IV, and V are primary triads and the ii, iii, and vi are secondary. The leading-tone triad, which he calls the "sub-tonic," is not a fundamental chord at all. York states that "it has no true root," thereby differing with Goetschius's theory that the vii is really a V7 with the root omitted. However, York does admit that "when used it is generally treated as if it were a V7 chord with the root omitted."[40]

Goetschius had stated that, besides modulation, tones foreign to the scale may be introduced by means of altered chords and mixed chords. York adds a third category, which he calls "chromatic chords." According to York, a chord subjected to ordinary alteration takes on a different form but retains the same "degree character," or diatonic function. For example, if the third of a IV triad in a major key is lowered, the form of the chord is changed to minor, but the chord still sounds and functions as a subdominant harmony.[41] However, in a chromatic chord, not only the form is changed but also the character of its function. In Figure 71, the II7, derived by raising the third of a ii7, is a chromatic chord; the alteration not only affects its form but also gives its function a dominant, rather than a supertonic, character. York stipulates that a chromatic chord must be followed by a characteristic chord of the key; otherwise, the effect is that of a modulation.[42] York's consciousness of the difference between formal character and functional character leads him to misgivings about Goetschius's concept of transient modulation (York's view on transient modulation will be mentioned in a later section).

Figure 71. A chromatic chord (York, p. 86)

York does not admit the augmented dominant seventh to the category of mixed chords. According to York, the only legitimate mixed chords are the French, German, and Italian augmented sixth-chords. Augmented sixth-chords appearing in other positions in the scale are to be regarded as being borrowed from another key. York states that mixed chords originate in the minor mode; therefore, the German sixth-chord in C should be spelled with E-flat, rather than D-sharp, regardless of the mode.[43]

To the elements borrowed from Goetschius's theory, York adds an original concept, which appears throughout his work. York attributes a special characteristic to each degree of the scale, thus:

Doh: firm, tone of rest, home
Ray: aspiring, expectant
Me: plaintive, quiet
Fah: solemn, desolate
Soh: bold, bright
Lah: sorrowful
Te: piercing, pressing upward.[44]

These characteristics are used to illustrate the composite characters of various chords. For instance, York analyzes the tonic triad as "the chord of rest (Doh), of quiet (Me), and yet it is a bright chord (Soh)."[45] The character of the subdominant triad is "solemn (Fah), restful (Doh), and inclined to sadness (Lah)."[46] However, York's system is less successful when applied to other chords. He has difficulty explaining, for instance, how the "solemn, desolate" Fah becomes the most active element of the dominant seventh-chord. He wisely refrains from attempting to explain why, in a ii[7] chord, the "restful" Doh has such an urgent downward tendency.

Goetschius's influence is also evident in the writing of Benjamin Cutter. Cutter was an active member of the musical community in Boston. After studying with Stephen Emery, Cutter taught theory and composition at the New England Conservatory, where he encountered Goetschius's theory.

Cutter's *Harmonic Analysis* was published in Boston in 1902. As the title implies, the work is intended as a textbook for analysis classes, rather than as an introduction to harmony.

Cutter lays great emphasis on the possibility of analyzing certain harmonic phenomena in various ways. He recommends that teachers and students remain open-minded in their analyses: "The class should enjoy the benefit of general discussions, and scholars should be led to argue for their figurings. But beware of narrow interpretations, of intolerant views; many phrases permit more than one solution."[47] Cutter's views on analysis also reflect his awareness of harmonic function. Repeatedly he recommends that the analyst take into account the behavior of a chord as well as its construction. "The identity of a chord depends on its resolution. In other words, judge a chord by what it does!"[48]

Goetschius's theory of natural progression by root movement of descending fifths appears in the introductory chapter of Cutter's work. After enumerating the possible root movements between chords (up or down a fifth, third, or second), Cutter states: "In that form of the Fifth-Relationship in which the root falls is found the most natural resolution or progression of any chord. Thus, the iii goes to the vi, the vi to the ii, the ii to the V, the V to the I, in both major and minor, and the nearer the progression approaches the tonic harmony, the more gratifying and reposeful the effect."[49] He does not mention that the root movement from VI to ii° in the minor mode is a descent of a diminished fifth, a considerably less normal or natural movement than that of the perfect fifth found in the other progressions. Also, he does not attempt to explain how the subdominant harmony fits into the scheme of descending fifths.

Although Cutter refers frequently to "principal" and "secondary" triads, he does not enumerate them specifically. However, he does imply the inclusion of Goetschius's second-dominant among the principal triads, stating: "The student will find that the I, IV, V, and ii . . . form the stock in trade of the composer and the material from which in Analysis he will have most often to consider."[50] Cutter deviates from Goetschius's theory by including the diminished triad on the leading tone in his list of triads in a key.[51]

Like Goetschius, Cutter considers the seventh-chord on the fifth and second degrees to be the most frequently used chords of the seventh. This leads Cutter to the curious conclusion that any nondominant seventh-chord is probably a ii7: "When a seventh chord does not contain the elements of V7—

major third, perfect fifth, minor seventh—nor of a vii $\overset{o}{7}_o$—minor third, diminished fifth, diminished seventh—this chord may be regarded as a supertonic seventh. In the great majority of cases this interpretation will be found correct, for the seventh chords on the other steps of the scale are rarely used save in sequence."[52]

Cutter adopts Goetschius's scheme of nearly related keys and goes a step further by insisting that all modulations be analyzed as transitions to nearly related keys: "If, for example, in C major the D major tonic appears after its dominant, the dominant must be marked as D minor and the major tonic as D major, involving a change of mode."[53] Cutter's recommended procedure for analyzing such modulations is a singular contradiction of his own rule, "The identity of a chord depends on its resolution."

Goetschius's influence is evident in Cutter's exposition of the nonharmonic tones. Cutter admits Goetschius's "suspension chord" as a nonharmonic phenomenon: "Suspensions may occur singly or in pairs; three voices may even be suspended at one time, or the whole chord be suspended rhythmically."[54] Similarly, Cutter acknowledges Goetschius's "anticipation chord" and gives the example in Figure 72.[55] Cutter also follows Goetschius by allowing an anticipation to prepare a suspension or retardation, as in Figure 73.[56] Like Goetschius, Cutter considers the escape tone to be a type of anticipation, provided that it appears as a member of the next chord, as in Figure 74a. If the tone is not a member of the chord, as is the case at b, Cutter calls it a "free tone."[57]

Figure 72. Bach (Cutter, p. 33)

Cutter extends Goetschius's definition of neighboring tones, or "embellishing notes," to include entire harmonic formations of such notes. He calls such a formation an

Figure 73.   Cutter, Etude *(Cutter, p. 35)*

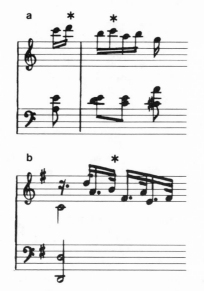

Figure 74.   Cutter, Etude *(Cutter, p. 34)*; Grieg, Op. 6 *(Cutter, p. 26)*

"embellishing chord" and states it "may form a definite chord, built up in thirds, or no chord at all. It may be diatonic or chromatic. Omit it and the essential chord will appear, visible to the eye."[58] However, he recommends that it be analyzed, when possible, as a chord, as well as an embellishment (see Figure 75, an example of Cutter's recommended analysis). Cutter mentions chords made up of clusters of passing-tones, which, of course, resemble Richter's "passing-chords." Cutter remarks: "Those chords which are passed through have no harmonic significance, and only the end chords need to be marked."[59] Another nonharmonic formation mentioned by Cutter is the "appoggiatura chord," which appears in an accented position and "has as its soprano a genuine appoggiatura."[60] An example of an appoggiatura chord is shown in Figure 76.

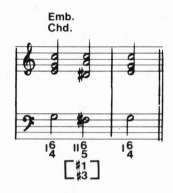

Figure 75.   *Embellishing chord (Cutter)*

Figure 76.   *Appoggiatura chord (Beethoven, Op. 14, no. 2)*

The period around 1900 is important as a formative era in the history of harmonic theory in America. During this time many of the ideas that American authors borrowed from Richter, Goetschius, and Prout assumed positions which they held long afterward in the body of common theoretical knowledge.

Richter's contributions to American harmonic theory are easily seen. Several of the features which Americans borrowed from Richter's system have been absorbed permanently into American theoretical usage. A modern analyst who uses uppercase and lowercase Roman numerals and the symbols ° and

⁺ to show whether chords are major, minor, diminished, or augmented is indebted to Weber and Richter for this system. When a teacher or a student of elementary theory harmonizes a simple diatonic melody with the primary triads I, IV, and V, knowing that these triads accommodate all the notes of the scale, he is acting on an observation that American theorists drew from Richter's system. If a theorist chooses to regard the leading-tone triad as an independent chord, rather than a part of the dominant harmony, he is following a practice that was introduced in the United States in the works of Weber and Richter.

It is more difficult to assess Prout's contributions. Although Prout's treatise on harmony had been available in the United States since 1889 and had been regarded by Americans as an authoritative work, it had no really consistent followers, with the possible exception of Spalding. Moreover, Prout himself had no important American students, as Richter and Jadassohn had.

The feature of the English system of theory that appears most frequently in American works is the "chord of nature." The several American authors who include in their works expositions of acoustical theory generally refer to the harmonic series as "nature's chord." Later followers of Goetschius, such as Franklin Robinson and Donald Tweedy, would include the concept of the "chord of nature" among their acoustical bases. The other important element of Prout's theory to survive in the United States is the concept of chords of the eleventh and thirteenth. While American theorists were not by any means convinced that eleventh- and thirteenth-chords were legitimate independent harmonies, they were at least aware of the notion.

Goetschius's most important contribution to the theoretical knowledge of the time, the theory of natural root progression by descending fifths, would persist as an essential feature in American harmony treatises. Its acceptance by American writers even in the 1890s, when it was still a relatively new idea, is a testimony to its importance. For the most part, it was simply accepted at the time. Later followers of Goetschius would try to solve its principal difficulty, the reconciliation of the subdominant with the pattern of descending fifths. However, by incorporating features of Goetschius's theory in their works, the American writers around 1900 began to break the tenure that

Richter's system had held in the United States. As early as 1904 Louis Elson was able to write: "Richter's rather too tyrannical grip was overthrown on this side of the ocean."[61]

Followers of Goetschius: Franklin Robinson, Donald Tweedy, George Wedge

Although American authors around 1900 had borrowed isolated features of Goetschius's theory, they had never taken over his entire system or developed it to any extent. Chadwick, Cutter, and others of the time were too immersed in Richter's system to abandon it completely, although they had no qualms about adopting such useful ideas as Goetschius's theory of harmonic progression.

The system of theory which Goetschius had proposed began to develop in its own right in the second decade of the twentieth century, and it reached its full vigor in the 1920s and early 1930s. Goetschius himself was teaching at the Institute of Musical Art in New York until 1925. It was there that his system was encountered by his colleague Franklin Robinson, who would develop a formidable speculative theory around it. Also, Goetschius's students at the Institute, notably Donald Tweedy and George Wedge, would use it as the basis of their own work in the practical sphere of harmonic theory.

Franklin Robinson was a student of Edward Mac-Dowell at Columbia University, where he received his M.A. in 1907. The following year he accepted the position of instructor at the Institute of Musical Art, where Goetschius was teaching. Robinson's treatise, *Aural Harmony*, first appeared in 1914, six years after he had begun teaching at the Institute, and was revised in 1936. It was intended as a textbook; however, it represents a speculative effort which is rare in American theoretical writing.

Although Robinson bases his presentation of harmony on acoustics, he is careful to state in the "Preface" to *Aural Harmony* that the "ideal" in music, like the ideal in any art, is not represented by precise conformance to the laws of physics: "If music were merely the disposition of tones accurately tuned to conform to the basic relationships of acoustics, would music be an art, or merely mathematical acoustics? There is in all art an element, a quality, or a characteristic—call it what you may—that transcends accuracy. Isn't it apparent that accuracy precludes two of the strongest elements of art, namely, imagination and individuality?"[62] Thus Robinson makes clear that discrepancies between natural intonation and humanly devised tuning systems are to be disregarded.

Robinson uses the harmonic series, extended to the sixteenth term, to divide tonal material into four classifications. The octave, the relationship resulting from the simplest division of the string, impresses the ear as being the same tone as the root but in a different register. Therefore, Robinson states, each octave tone of the root in a harmonic series takes on the qualities of the original root. That is, each octave tone becomes a new root tone. Each root tone, then, represents a new classification, as shown in Figure 77.[63] According to Robinson this system of classification is not man-made but natural: "we find that in music Nature classifies by re-iteration of characteristics, just as she does in zoology."[64]

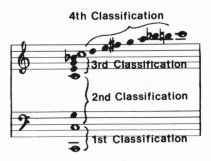

Figure 77.   Classifications in the harmonic series (Robinson, 1:1)

Because the octave is merely a repetition of the original pitch in a different register, Robinson deduces that the First Classification simply demonstrates highness and lowness. The Second Classification presents "the first true tonal relationships of music, one consisting of two tones of different pitch—C and G."[65] Thus, the concept of interval is introduced, as the perfect fifth and perfect fourth appear. Robinson has difficulty deciding whether the G between the two C's should be considered a root tone. He establishes the fifth and fourth as inversions of each other by noting that the fifth, G, is a diatonic member of the scale of C, and the upper tone of the fourth, C, is a diatonic member of the G scale. In doing so he observes that "the lower tones of both intervals are here considered root-tones of major scales."[66] Immediately, however, he changes his stance by stating that the fifth, C–G, is based on the real root tone C, whereas "the lower G of the perfect fourth G–C is not a real root-tone, obviously, not being a re-iteration of the fundamental tone C."[67] He presently changes his mind again: "The perfect fifth in the Second Classification is an interval composed of two root-tones."[68] In fact, Robinson has a great deal of trouble deciding what constitutes a "root tone." The E in the Third Classification is at first not considered a root tone, logically, since it is not a repetition of the original C. Yet, in discussing the major triad, Robinson writes: "The third of the triad is the characteristic tone of the lower root-tone and at the same time the root-tone of the upper third."[69]

The Third Classification introduces the concept of harmony, and the Fourth Classification presents the scale. Robinson defines the triad as "a structure built upon a root-tone and composed of two thirds that differ in character, one major and one minor."[70] For this reason the augmented and diminished "triads" are not to be regarded as triads at all but as formations implying chaos.[71] Robinson notes that the B-flat in the Third Classification forms with the C above it what appears to be a major second, an interval properly belonging in the Fourth Classification. He explains that the true major second 8:9 is given by the pitches C–D in the Fourth Classification and that the interval from B-flat to C is 7:8, actually a bit larger than a major second—a curious distinction in a theory renouncing acoustical accuracy.

The Fourth Classification presents the scale, including an F-sharp and a B-flat. Robinson changes the F-sharp to F-natural because "F-sharp is an inaccurate representation of this overtone."[72] So, of course, is F-natural. He determines the F-natural by measuring a perfect fourth up from C. The fourth scale degree is thus a perfect fourth above, or inverted, a perfect fifth below the tonic. The B-flat is discarded because he considers it a tone of the scale of F, despite the fact that it has appeared twice in the harmonic series of C.[73]

Goetschius's theory enters into the explanation of the

Fourth Classification. Robinson states that the tones C, E, and G (and B-flat) are harmonic tones, since they are reiterated from the Third Classification; the other tones, D, F (or F-sharp?), A, and B-natural, are nonharmonic, or active, tones. Each active tone has a tendency to resolve to a harmonic tone: B resolves to C, A to G, F to E, and D to C or E. Robinson adds that these tendencies are affected not only by the proximity of an active tone to its rest tone of resolution, but also by the degree of counter-attraction exerted by the rest tone on the other side of it. For instance, B is separated from C by a semitone, as is F from E. However, the G beneath the B is two whole tones distant from it and thus exerts relatively little counter-attraction. B thus resolves to C more easily than does F to E, because F is only one whole tone distant from its counter-attracting rest tone G.[74]

Robinson presents a remarkable theory of the derivation of the minor scale. He admits that the minor mode is "less natural" than the major; nonetheless, he reverts to the harmonic series for his explanation. Assuming a series of "undertones" (an idea that had been tried by a number of European theorists, notably Riemann, and abandoned due to its physical impossibility), Robinson discovers his "minor scale" in the Fourth Classification below the original root tone, as shown in Figure 78. From this, he deduces that the only legitimate form of the minor scale is its Aeolian form: "It is most illuminating to observe that the melodic form of the minor scale includes the flat 7th step, the flat 6th step, and the flat 3rd step of the minor scale as melodic tones of Nature's minor scale."[75] Less illuminating, of course, is nature's presentation of a flat fifth step and two forms of the second step. Moreover, he does not explain why he disregards the first three classifications of "undertones." Of

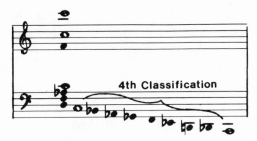

4th Classification

Figure 78. Derivation of the minor scale (Robinson, 1:193)

course, had he considered them, he would have had to designate the first, second, fourth, and sixth degrees of the minor scale the tones of rest, and perhaps even regard F–A-flat–C as the tonic triad of C minor.

Robinson insists that melodic activity and harmonic motion belong to two separate planes (he illustrates this by proposing three-dimensional music staff-paper; the vertical plane accommodates melodic tones, and the horizontal plane shows movement of chord roots[76]). The tones of the major scale, when considered as chord roots, are related by the interval of the fifth, "the simplest pitch-relation in music." Like Goetschius, Robinson erects a series of fifths up from C to include G, D, A, E, and possibly B, and one downward fifth to F.[77] He explains that, while the tones above C are derived from the division of the length of a vibrating string, the F is produced by adding a segment to the string, so that the original length is now two-thirds of the total length. He apparently realizes that the process of "string-addition" is acoustically inadmissible, for he states that the tone C is responsible "in a less natural manner, for the exotic tone F."[78] He recognizes that in his scheme of harmonic progression he cannot place the F a fifth beneath C, as F would then usurp the function of tonic from C. He says: "We shall have to experiment regarding the position of the tone F in relation to all of the other tones in order to find out how this less natural tone is interrelated with them. I shall, however, defer this experiment until later in this chapter."[79] He places the triad IV between the II and the VI in his pattern of harmonic progression, as illustrated in Figure 79, and never again refers to its peculiar position.

Figure 79.   Robinson, 1:41

Robinson does provide an explanation of sorts for the progression IV–V. The root movement is not that of an ascending second, as at *a* in Figure 80, but rather of a descending seventh, as at *b*, with the root of V transferred up an octave for the sake of voice-leading.[80]

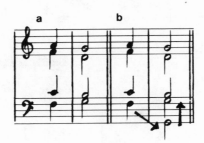

Figure 80. Robinson, 1:47

Robinson's treatment of diatonic harmony owes much to Goetschius. Every chord root except the tonic is considered an active root, and its normal progression is to the chord rooted a fifth below, with the exception of the progression VI–IV–II. As the progression approaches its goal of the tonic, the degree of intensity of activity increases.[81] The tonic itself is, of course, a static chord. Thus it may not be made into an active harmony by such means as the addition of a seventh.[82]

Goetschius's influence is also evident in Robinson's exposition of chromatic harmony. Robinson states that chromatic alterations are not natural phenomena but are humanly conceived. Thus, these chromatic changes must not disturb the natural harmonic progression: "We will find that he [man] cannot imperiously disregard the way in which the triad, in its diatonic form, serves the key. For example, he cannot disregard the rest quality of the I triad by chromatically altering any of its tones, thereby transforming the chord to become active in character; or again, he cannot disregard the meaning of the V triad and chromatically alter its root-tone."[83] Robinson therefore limits chromatic alteration to only certain tones in each chord (see Figure 81). The similarity of Robinson's symbolization of alterations to Goetschius's should be noted. From the altered scale degrees in these chords, Robinson deduces the spellings of the major and minor chromatic scales, shown in Figure 82.

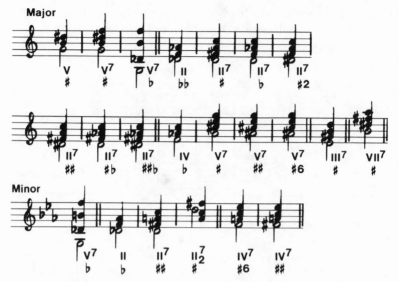

Figure 81.   Chromatic alterations (Robinson, Vol. 2)

Figure 82.   Robinson, 2:59, 51

Robinson's exposition of nonharmonic tones results in a system quite different from Goetschius's. Robinson states that there are two types of nonharmonic tones: those that replace members of the harmony, and those that do not. The sole member of the former category is the appoggiatura. Robinson's definition of the appoggiatura is an interesting foreshadowing of Walter Piston's idea: an appoggiatura is any nonharmonic tone that occurs on an accented beat and resolves downward. Thus, the accented passing tone and the suspension (tied or not to its preparation) are types of appoggiatura.[84] The nonharmonic tones that do not replace chord tones include the neighboring tone (of which the passing tone is a type) and the anticipation.[85] Robinson includes the organ point in his exposition of nonharmonic tones but states that he really considers it to be a harmonic phenomenon: "We have previously seen that a tone in the bass voice of a chord structure is continuously endeavoring to assert itself as a root-tone; the organ-point succeeds. Throughout its entire length it constantly imposes upon the chord structures that occur above it the intensity it possesses as a root-tone."[86]

Robinson does not consider chords of the ninth to be legitimate harmonic formations but calls them "appoggiatura chords."[87] In the chord in Figure 83a, the A is not a chord ninth but an appoggiatura replacing the tone G in the uppermost voice. The A is symbolized in the analysis by its scale-degree number 6, placed beneath the Roman numeral. Similarly, at *b* the appoggiatura E is shown as the third scale degree. Appoggiatura chords may also appear on the chord roots VI, III, and VII.

Figure 83.   Robinson, 1:66

Although parts of Robinson's theory are faulty, he was respected by American theorists of the 1920s as an authority in the field of speculative theory. Several of his ideas, including his concept of the appoggiatura, are ahead of their time in the development of American theory. Also, Robinson is the first American theorist to emphasize the dominant character of the precadential second-inversion tonic chord.[88] He also considers classical sonata-allegro form to be a two-part form dependent on modulation from the tonic to the dominant and back; popular works of formal theory of the period, such as those of Goetschius and Prout, classify sonata as a ternary form.

Robinson's attempt to solve the principal difficulty of Goetschius's theory of harmonic progression—the reconciliation of the subdominant with the pattern of descending fifths—failed because Robinson neglected to provide any explanation of his reasoning. Appearing in the wake of Robinson's theory, however, was a more conscientious attempt to solve the mystery of the subdominant, namely, Otto Ortmann's article "Notes on the Nature of Harmony" in *Musical Quarterly* (1921). Ortmann constructs the series of fifths upward from C and places a triad in C major on each tone, as shown in Figure 84*a*. (The letters M, O, Q, S, and U are simply Ortmann's labels for the purpose of discussion of the diagram.) The natural progression of harmony is, of course, toward the tonic at U. He then introduces another interval into his theory:

> The basic interval of chord structure . . . is not a fifth, but a third. Accordingly, the third is a harmonic interval. It cannot be primary because it is not present in the original series of fifths. . . . But it can be secondary because the chords which we built upon the single tones of [Figure 84*a*] contain not only a fifth, but also the interval of a third. By placing triads in third-relationships to those already derived, we get as our complete chordal series [the chords shown at *b*].[89]

The omission of third-related triads between O and P and between R and S appears to be due to his own inadvertence. The added triads N, Q, and T are termed "secondary triads." Ortmann states that, because they are not components of the fifth-progression, the secondary triads are not considered independent harmonies, but seventh-chords with omitted roots. Thus the G triad at N is actually a III7 with the root omitted, as opposed to the true V triad at S.

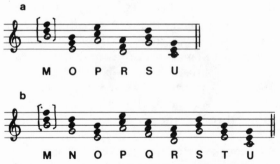

Figure 84. Ortmann (Musical Quarterly, 1921), p. 368

To this point, Ortmann's presentation indicates that the IV is actually an incomplete II7, which he says it sometimes is:

"Any chord progression such as Q–S–U is good, because Q, being harmonically R, produces the perfect primary progression R–S–U."[90] However, his procedure cannot be applied as successfully to other portions of his progression. By analogy, the progression II–V–III (R–S–T) ought to form a satisfactory cadence, because III at T is a tonic seventh, without its root, and is thus harmonically U.

But according to Ortmann the IV used as an incomplete II7 is quite different in function from the IV used as a true subdominant. An example of the latter is the plagal cadence. He considers that in such a circumstance the IV's function is actually melodic, rather than harmonic. That is, the IV is really a conglomeration of nonharmonic tones relating to the notes of the tonic harmony. The true subdominant is thus harmonically a part of the I. To support this, Ortmann points out that the success of a plagal cadence really depends upon a preceding dominant-tonic progression: "The progression IV–I is really only felt as IV–I when it has been preceded by some V–I progression. Played alone, without accent, IV-I is usually felt as I–V."[91] In any case, Ortmann insists that there is no real fifth-relation between I and IV. "As long as we . . . speak of harmonic relations, such as the subdominant, where no harmonic relation exists, we cannot hope to arrive at any satisfactory conclusions."[92]

In the realm of practical harmony, Robinson's development of Goetschius's theory appears in Donald Tweedy's *Manual of Harmonic Technic*, published in 1928. Tweedy had been a student of Goetschius and Robinson at the Institute of Musical Art and was subsequently appointed to teach theory at the Eastman School of Music. Tweedy's *Manual* was the result of the system of teaching which he developed at Eastman. He dedicated the book to Goetschius.

A unique pedagogical feature of Tweedy's work is the deliberate avoidance of statements of rules of harmonic theory. The *Manual* was at first advertised as "the theory text without rules."[93] In the Preface Tweedy explains his aim: "I hope there is no dogma in these pages. I have chosen rather to address numerous questions to the student, designed to elicit from him his own harmonic theory."[94] Even so, many of the questions that Tweedy addresses to the student betray the influence which he attributes to the work of Goetschius, Ernst Bloch, and especially Franklin Robinson, of whom he says, "To the last named must be accorded particularly deep appreciation for the inspiration of his personal training which, though frequently spiced by the zest of emphatic disagreement with his ideas, was always evocative of fruitful discussion."[95]

Of course, any theory that is directly influenced by Goetschius must establish the perfect fifth as the interval of greatest significance. Tweedy does so in his first chapter, entitled "Preliminaries." His presentation of the fifth is based not only on acoustics but also on ethnomusicology, a field that was just beginning to attract interest in the United States in 1928.[96] After establishing the fifth as being represented by the proportion 2:3, Tweedy astutely observes: "All systems of arrangement which have had artistic vitality agree on one point: they include a tone corresponding to that of a vibrating body two-thirds the length of that producing the original fundamental."[97]

In addition to the perfect fifth, Tweedy seeks to establish the importance of the major third, again by reverting to an ethnomusicological basis:

> We find, in the examination of various folk-scales, a widespread use of a five-tone scale corresponding to C–D–E–G–A–(C) in the major scale of seven tones. This scale is called pentatonic (Greek: meaning five-tone) and the interesting points about it are that it contains a Tonic and a Dominant with the pitches one whole-tone above both, *plus* another pitch two whole-tones above the Tonic. . . . The science of acoustics bears out this primitive instinct for a major third, as the interval C to E corresponds to the next simplest mathematical ratio (4:5) after those producing the octave and the fifth.[98]

Although Tweedy does not specify which folk-scales he is considering, his statement regarding the third is not strictly accurate. To cite a well-known example, the Chinese pentatonic scale, calculated by the Huang Chung theory, uses a series of acoustically correct fifths in a manner similar to the Pythagorean procedure. Thus, a Chinese major third is actually of the proportion 64:81. Chinese musicians have never seriously considered adjusting their third to the simpler proportion 4:5; in fact, they have systematically resisted all attempts to alter the original Huang Chung tuning. Many African pentatonic scales contain major thirds which are almost a quarter-tone flatter than the third 4:5. The original pentatonic scales of Scotland and

Ireland have, over the centuries, been influenced first by the ecclesiastical modes (which themselves were calculated by the Pythagorean system) and later by the major scale, whose tuning resulted from a need for a major third 4:5 for harmonic purposes. Tweedy continues:

> But there is another form of pentatonic scale found especially among Celtic peoples in which a different arrangement is met with. This runs A–B–D–E–G–(A), or, expressed with C as the Tonic, C–D–F–G–B–flat–(C). There is no third in this scale, and the note below both Tonic and Dominant is a whole-step away. When a third is added, it is apt to be a half-tone above D (a minor third from the Tonic): when a sixth is added, it is indifferently a half- or a whole-tone above G.
>
> These two pentatonic scales show a very ancient difference of feeling between Dominants. The true Dominant of the second form seems to be F rather than G, the Dominant *below* (Subdominant). This note is to C as 3:2, another simple mathematical relationship.[99]

This is a curious statement. It appears that Tweedy is attempting to establish the subdominant as a peculiarity to the minor mode. He states that "in the main, the distinction seems to be that, for a bright mood, the Western singer chooses the upper Dominant, with major third, and 'natural' half-step below the Tonic . . . for a dark mood, he chooses the lower Dominant, with minor third and 'flat' whole-step below the Tonic."[100] But this is not the case, nor has it ever been considered to be so, either by Western theorists or by practicing musicians. Both the upper and lower dominants are considered as such in both major and minor modes. The size of the third above the tonic does not cause the fifth above the tonic to cease acting as a dominant. Even in Tweedy's own example of a "minor" pentatonic song, the Irish *caoine* (keen, or funeral lament) shown in Figure 85, the G is more firmly established as a dominant than the F.

In addition to the dominant and the subdominant, Tweedy presents the second-dominant, Goetschius's term for the second scale-degree used as a chord root. This gives him the framework of the scale: "The invariable constituents of a scale may be said to be, then, the Tonic and its three Dominants, Dominant proper, Subdominant, and Second Dominant. The variable constituents are the third tone above (the Mediant), the

Och-och-one ———————— Och-och- och-one

Och-och-och-och-one ———————— Och-och-one ———

Figure 85. Caoine, *from Joyce,* Ancient Irish Music *(Tweedy, p. 6)*

third below (Submediant), and the tone directly below the Tonic."[101] Tweedy admits all three forms of the minor scale as legitimate forms.

Tweedy presents the harmonic series as the model after which harmony is constructed. Giving a chart of the harmonic series extended to the sixteenth term, as in Figure 86, he poses questions to the student:

What three-tone chord would be nearest to an acoustical ideal, i.e., what combination of three different pitches would be in accordance

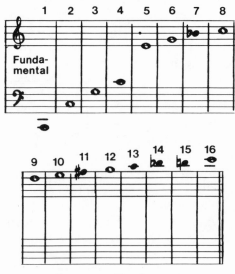

Figure 86. Tweedy, p. 19

with the natural phenomenon of overtones?—What combination of four?—Of five? . . . Considering all of the overtones of the fundamental C as if they were in tune from the standpoint of the tempered scale, which three form the major triad?—The diminished triad?—The minor triad?—The augmented triad?[102]

The last several of his questions may lead the student to some unusual ideas about acoustical theory. For instance, the minor triad, traditionally represented by the proportion 10:12:15, may be seen in Tweedy's chart as the sixth, seventh, and ninth harmonics, if one "considers all the overtones of the fundamental C as if they were in tune from the standpoint of the tempered scale."

Tweedy lists the triads that occur in a major key, including the diminished triad VII, and presents his statement concerning harmonic progression: "If all the triads in the Key are used in succession, the order is apt to be: VII→III→VI→IV→II→V→I. . . ."[103] He illustrates the roots of the "indicated succession," as shown in Figure 87. He then poses his questions:

What is the mathematical relationship of the pitch G to the pitch C, whether in length of resonant medium or in number of vibrations per second?—Can you apply this ratio to the entire succession of pitches? —Where will it fail?—If one pitch is omitted will the ratio apply throughout?—What is the ratio of the pitch of the omitted note to C? —Can you find this omitted note in the Table of Overtones from C?— Could you find C among the overtones reckoned from the pitch of the omitted note?—Is that note important in the melodic scale?—If the ratio of that note were again applied, what note would be reached?—Is this note in the scale of C?—To what general conclusion do you come concerning the harmonic relationship of the pitches forming the scale of C?[104]

C:

Figure 87. Tweedy, p. 21

Thus Tweedy lays before the student the thorniest problem of Goetschius's theory: the placement of the subdominant. Tweedy's questions indicate that he prefers that the subdominant be regarded as the fifth below the tonic. If so, why does he place it between the VI and the II in his scheme of harmonic progression? Robinson had proposed this order of progression, but he had never explained his placement of the subdominant, and neither does Tweedy.

Tweedy's acknowledgment of the triad on VII is a departure from both Goetschius's and Robinson's theories. Tweedy actually considers the VII triad to have two possible meanings. It may be a "true" VII, which resolves to the III, the next chord in Tweedy's progression; or it may be a "dominant" VII, which acts as an incomplete V7 by resolving to the tonic.[105] Thus the VII may be either very distant from the tonic center or very close to it.

From his exposition of harmonic progression, Tweedy develops a scheme of functional harmony which is remarkably similar to Goetschius's. Tweedy considers all harmony in a key to belong to one of three classes, which he represents as I, V, and II. "It should be remembered that I means 'Tonic Class' chord (including VI as a deceptive resolution of V, and possibly III as incomplete tonic-seventh), that V includes VII as a dominant, and that II stands for any chord which may precede the dominant—which is 'out beyond V' in tonality."[106] While Goetschius would not have agreed with the idea of a "tonic seventh" chord, he certainly would have no difficulty accepting Tweedy's concept of functional harmony in general.

For analysis of diatonic harmony, Tweedy employs Goetschius's symbols faithfully; only uppercase Roman numerals are used, and inversions are shown by the subscript arabic numerals 1, 2, and 3. However, to show the presence of accidentals, Tweedy abandons Goetschius's sharps and flats in favor of a system of acute and grave accent marks. A raised tone in a diatonic chord in the minor mode is shown with an acute accent mark placed above the Roman numeral; for instance, V́ represents the dominant triad with the raised third in a minor key. A chromatically raised tone in a chord is shown by an acute accent placed beneath the Roman numeral; a chromatically flattened tone is indicated by a grave accent similarly placed. In most instances Tweedy does follow Goetschius's practice of forcing the reader to deduce which chord member has been altered. He gives an example: "When only the 2nd scale step is lowered in the V7, the symbol will be Ṿ7. And when both 2 and 4 are lowered, the symbol will be Ṿ7 (minor mode only). But if 4 be lowered without also lowering 2,the symbol is V́7 with 4́ written underneath."[107] The use of acute and grave accent marks is intended to facilitate class exercises in harmonic dictation; it may well do this, but it does not solve the most serious deficiency of Goetschius's symbols for chromatic alteration.

Tweedy's treatment of altered chords follows Goetschius's and Robinson's to a great extent. Tweedy states that chromatic alterations must not interfere with the functional behavior of the chord. The specific alterations that he permits are mostly similar to Robinson's, and even when Tweedy diverges he presents Robinson's idea on the point in question. For example, Tweedy shows the progression in Figure 88, and asks: "Are the first three chords of [Figure 88] to be analyzed as C: I F: V̦ I or as C: I I IV ?—Many theorists do not permit the second analysis, and declare that there can be no chromatic alteration in the I. What is your opinion?"[108]

Figure 88.   Tweedy, p. 236

In connection with chromatic harmony Tweedy introduces what he calls "color-chords" and describes them thus: "Occasionally we meet with passages in music which defy analysis for tonality or key. The chords involved have no discernible function in relation to a key-centre."[109] Into the category of color-chords fall all the harmonies that are used for no other purpose than color. Tweedy analyzes these by species. For instance, if a color-chord of three notes were to form a major triad (directly or enharmonically), it would be considered a First-Species triad. Minor-triad formations constitute the Second Species, and augmented triads make up the Third Species,

diminished triads the Fourth. Seventh- and ninth-chord formations are organized into similar systems of species. To symbolize
a color-chord Tweedy uses a two-digit figure: the first digit
shows whether the chord is a triad or a seventh- or ninth-chord,
and the second digit indicates the species. A minor triad used as a
color-chord would thus be marked 32; the 3 indicating it is a triad,
the 2 indicating the Second (minor) Species. An inverted color-
chord is indicated by means of Goetschius's subscript inversion-
numeral placed in the position of the denominator; if a minor
color-chord were to appear in first inversion, for instance, it
would be symbolized $\frac{32}{1}$. The absence of any Roman numeral is
especially appropriate, since no diatonic function is thus
attributed to the color-chord.

Tweedy illustrates color-chords with Bach's har-
monization of the chorale "Ach Gott und Herr," a representative
passage of which is shown in Figure 89. In this passage the chords
at *b*, marked $\frac{71}{1}$, are probably best analyzed, as Tweedy does, as

Figure 89. Bach, Chorale "Ach Gott und Herr" (Tweedy, p. 34)

color-chords. Although the individual parts at *b* perform linear functions, the harmonies that they form do not function diatonically at all. It is strange that Tweedy must identify the chord at *a* as a color-chord, since this chord is part of a series of root movements of descending fifths. The analysis shown in Figure 90, using the principle of transient modulation, might be a more representative interpretation, since it at least shows the fifth-progression from the chord on B-flat to the dominant of A-flat. The idea of analyzing nonfunctional chords as color-chords is a useful one, but the analyst must take care not to abuse it. It should not be turned into a catch-all category for any chords that seem to "defy analysis."

Figure 90. Bach, "Ach Gott und Herr"

Tweedy's exposition of nonharmonic tones shows Robinson's influence. Like Robinson, Tweedy classifies nonharmonic tones into those that intervene between two chord tones and those that are used in association with a single chord tone.[110] Tweedy considers the latter category to include the auxiliary tone and the appoggiatura, of which the suspension is a type. The changing-tone figure may belong to either category. Tweedy states that in the changing-tone figure the final return to the chord tone may be omitted; the result is a form of escape tone.

More conventional than Tweedy's *Manual* in its pedagogical approach is the work of another prominent Goetschius student, George Wedge. After his studies at the Institute of Musical Art, Wedge held teaching positions at New York University and the Curtis Institute of Music. In 1938 he became the dean of the Institute of Musical Art, which by this time had become a part of the Julliard School of Music. He authored an impressive array of books, including *Ear Training and Sight-Singing* (1921), *Advanced Ear Training and Sight-Singing* (1922), *Applied Harmony* (1930–1932, 2 vols.), and *The Gist of Music* (1936).

It is interesting to compare his early writings with the more mature theory found in *Applied Harmony*. In the early work *Advanced Ear Training and Sight-Singing*, for instance, he presents a great deal of harmonic theory, practically all of which is drawn unmodified from Goetschius's system. The natural root-progression by fifths, the treatment of diatonic harmony, including triads and seventh- and ninth-chords, the chromatic alterations of only specific scale degrees, transient modulation— all of these and other features of Goetschius's work are faithfully presented in *Advanced Ear Training*, even down to such details as the "Stride."[111] Wedge's only divergence is his placement of the IV triad between the II and the VI, a feature borrowed from Robinson; even in this instance his explanation echoes Goetschius: "In arranging the chords the IV is transposed and placed between the II and the VI, as the II7 chord includes the IV and is nearer the key-centre."[112]

By 1930, however, Wedge had developed somewhat more independent views on harmonic theory. These may be found in *Applied Harmony*. While this work is still strongly based on Goetschius's system, Wedge introduces his own modifications, notably those regarding harmonic progression, chromatic harmony, modulation, and analytical symbols. *Applied Harmony* is Wedge's contribution to the development of the Goetschius tradition.

Wedge begins his exposition with the familiar demonstration of the perfect fifth:

> Given a string that vibrates to give the pitch Middle C, to find the tone most nearly related in vibrations but different in sound, first divide the string in half. . . . Using the next ratio, thirds, divide the string into thirds and set the large segment to vibrating and it will produce the tone G, a perfect fifth above C. Therefore, the nearest related tone to any other tone and differing in pitch will be the fifth above.[113]

Using the fifth as a unit of measurement, he constructs series not only up from C but also down to obtain the tones shown in Figure 91. From this series of fifth-related pitches, a selection is made of the tones that form the material of the scale and key. The choice consists of the tonic, the five tones above it, and the single tone beneath it. The keys of C and G are formed as they appear in Figure 92.

Figure 91.   Wedge, 1:1

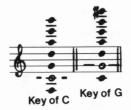

Key of C   Key of G

Figure 92.   Wedge, 1:2

Wedge's presentation of the derivation of the key material is thus identical to Goetschius's theory of tone-relations, and it poses the same problem. If, as Wedge says, "the nearest related tone to any tone . . . is the fifth above," how does one account for the single fifth *below* the keynote? Wedge, more than any other post-Goetschius theorist, uses the fifth as a static unit of measurement. But the acoustically derived fifth has not only dimension but also a strong implication of direction; this is illustrated clearly by Goetschius's use of the fifth in his theory of harmonic progression. The perfect fifth is not a "two-way" interval. Admittedly, the subdominant tone is associable with the tonic, in that the tonic is its most nearly related tone. However, the formation of tonality begins with the tonic, and it is impossible to find the subdominant, or any "undertone," among the tones related to the tonic, because these related tones are "fifths above," as Wedge states. He seems to be aware that the arrangement of fifths around the tonic is a peculiar one, for he suggests factors to account for this arrangement: "How this choice was made is not definitely known, but it was obviously influenced by the arrangement of the tones in the modal scale, by the distribution of tones among the consonant overtones, and by the tones which meet the requirements of the tempered tuning of the modern piano keyboard."[114] Of these three factors, the only one that explains the acceptance of the subdominant is the scale's development from the ecclesiastical modes, calculated by the Pythagorean system.

Like Goetschius, Wedge considers the minor scale to be an alteration of the major. He admits all three types of the minor scale as legitimate forms.[115]

In his presentation of the triads of a key, Wedge includes the VII as an independent chord. He qualifies this by stating that the VII is not much used in its root position, and that in first inversion it generally substitutes for the V chord and may thus be used to form an authentic cadence.[116]

Wedge's presentation of harmonic progression is somewhat more complicated than Goetschius's. Wedge first presents progression by root-movements of fifths toward the tonic:

> Chords are built upon the tones of the key. These tones are related in fifths, starting with the key-note, which is the key-centre and at rest. The other tones are active, and their activity varies in intensity according to their proximity to the key-centre. It is a law of gravity that falling particles increase in activity until they come to rest. Therefore, as soon as any one of these active chords is used, it will progress to a more active chord until it comes to rest upon the I chord, the key-centre.[117]

The progression of any chord to a more active chord is termed the "normal" progression (shown in Figure 93), and a root movement in the opposite direction is said to be "irregular" or "regressive" movement (he is careful to avoid the term "progression" when referring to regressive movement).

The root movement of a descending fifth, however, is not the only "normal" progression that he presents. Also possible are "normal" progressions by thirds: "The normal progression of chord-roots down in thirds gives the I–VI–IV–II–(VII)–V–(III)–

Figure 93. Wedge, 1:39

I." The VII is parenthesized because it is rarely used in root
position; the III is often omitted from the progression because "it
sounds as if the root of the III chord is an anticipation of the I
chord which follows."[118] It is perhaps for this reason that he
considers the ascending third-progression III–V to be a "normal"
progression. The "normal" movements of roots by seconds are
the progressions III–IV, IV–V, VI–V, III–II, and II–I.

Figure 94. Normal progressions (Wedge, 1:40–41)

In each root movement shown in Figure 94, Wedge
follows his own rule of progressing from a less active chord to
one that is more active in the scheme of descending fifths. Some
of the progressions are even comprehensible in terms of
Goetschius's theory. The progression at *b* is easily explainable,
assuming that the VII and III are omitted: the tonic and
subdominant triads are each followed by their relative secondary
chords, and the progression II–V–I is natural (the progression at
b also fits perfectly into Robinson's pattern). However, several of
the progressions depend on the elision of chords in the series of
fifths, a process which Wedge does not mention. The progression
at *c*, for instance, requires the elision of two chords, the VI and
the II. The progression at *h* skips nothing less than the dominant
chord. The progressions at *c, g,* and *h* are rarely used in musical

practice. It might be expected that Wedge would elaborate on his reasons for considering them "normal" progressions. Instead he says, "The choice of root-progressions depends entirely upon what is to be expressed, and the form through which the expression is made."[119]

The seventh-chords recognized by Wedge are shown in Figure 95. These include every possible diatonic seventh-chord in the major and harmonic minor scales. Thus, unlike most theorists of the time, Wedge includes in his list chords that involve major sevenths, shown at *a, b,* and *c.* These he calls "large" seventh-chords. The symbol for a large seventh-chord is L7 preceded by either a plus or minus sign. The symbol for a half-diminished seventh-chord is the "diminished" symbol ° with a stroke through it, thus: ⌀.[120] Wedge appears to be the first American theorist to use the term "half-diminished seventh." He states that the normal resolution of a seventh-chord is to the chord rooted a fifth below.

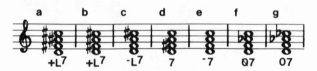

Figure 95.   *Seventh-chords (Wedge, 1:109)*

Wedge's analytical symbols show a departure from the Goetschius tradition. Wedge presents Goetschius's method of showing inversions with subscript numerals but seems to prefer the practice of combining the Roman numerals with the figured-bass symbols. To show chord roots without respect to a particular key, Wedge revives Weber's idea by using the appropriate letter followed, if necessary, by a figured-bass symbol or a subscript numeral. The chord in Figure 96 may be symbolized any of the four ways shown.

Wedge's most radical departure from Goetschius's theory occurs in the treatment of chromatic harmony. Wedge considers that chromatic harmonies may be used not only as substitutes for diatonic chords but also as embellishments of them. His "embellishing chords" include chords now known as secondary dominants, as well as the augmented sixth-chords. Since "embellishing chords" constitute Wedge's solution to the

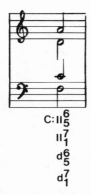

$$C: \text{II}^6_5$$
$$\text{II}^7_1$$
$$d^6_5$$
$$d^7_1$$

Figure 96. Analytical symbols (Wedge)

problem of transient modulation, examination of them will be deferred until the next section.

Wedge presents several types of chromatic chords which act as substitutes for diatonic harmonies. The most common type is the "borrowed" chord. In a major key, the lowered third, sixth, and seventh scale degrees may be borrowed from the parallel minor mode. Similarly, the minor key may borrow the raised third, sixth, and seventh degrees from the major.[121] Another type of chromatic chord occurs when the II, III, or VI is changed from minor to major in a major key. The II of the minor mode may also be changed to major.[122] The major triad formed on the lowered second-scale degree, the Neapolitan chord, is also possible. Wedge symbolizes it with a section mark (§).[123] Also, a dominant triad or dominant seventh-chord may appear in augmented form, with the fifth raised. Wedge's symbol for the augmented dominant is a dagger (†), which is conveniently similar to Richter's plus-sign symbol (+) for the augmented chord.[124]

Wedge admits five types of nonharmonic tones: the passing tone, the neighboring tone, the suspension, the anticipation, and the appoggiatura. He makes no attempt to consolidate these into larger classifications, as Robinson and Tweedy had done. Wedge permits Goetschius's "harmonic suspension" and "harmonic anticipation": "An entire chord may be suspended by repeating or tying it from an unaccented to an accented pulse . . . . An entire chord may be used as an anticipation."[125]

It should not be supposed that Goetschius's influence in the 1920s and 1930s was limited to the work of his students. Although Tweedy and Wedge represent the most important development of the practical aspects of Goetschius's theory, its influence was felt by all American theorists of the time. In fact, it is difficult to examine any harmony text of the period without discovering evidence of Goetschius's influence. In George Leighton's *Harmony, Analytical and Applied* (1927), for example, one finds an extended discussion of the active and inactive tones of the scale, the chromatic alteration of only certain scale degrees, and the statement that the IV triad is really a part of the supertonic harmony.[126] In *The Texture of Music* (1931), by Carl Paige Wood (a student of Walter Spalding), one reads that the leading-tone chord is actually a manifestation of the dominant harmony. Wood also attaches great importance to the concept of active and inactive tones.[127] The active and inactive scale degrees appear in 1933 in Carleton Bullis's remarkably original *Harmonic Forms*.[128]

It is probably fitting that the final development of the Goetschius theory during this period was presented, in 1934, by its author, Percy Goetschius. Now living in retirement in New Hampshire, Goetschius was still actively writing books and articles on music. In *The Structure of Music* (1934) Goetschius once more advances an explanation of tonality.

Goetschius's explanation of 1934 is based on the concept of "nucleus tones." From a keynote C, a series of four acoustically correct fifths is projected upward, producing the tones G, D, A, and E above the C. These five tones form the nucleus of the key. By extending the pattern an additional fifth in each direction, the tones F and B are obtained (see Figure 97). Although the F and the B are members of the scale, they are excluded as harmonic roots; Goetschius states that only the "nucleus tones" can be roots of chords. Thus, the triad VII is really an incomplete V7, and the IV is an incomplete II7. [129]

Figure 97.   *Nucleus tones* (*Goetschius,* The Structure of Music)

The theory presented in *The Structure of Music* is no more than a clarification of the theory proposed in *The Material Used in Musical Composition* in 1889. The "nucleus tones" represent the tonic and the four active classes of harmony in Goetschius's original system. The subdominant tone and the leading tone are accepted as melodic factors but are prevented from figuring as roots in the harmonic progression; the VII is too distant from the tonic, and the IV is on the wrong side of the tonic. Thus, these two harmonies must be explained in terms of one or another of the four classes, or "nucleus tones."

The Problem of Transient Modulation

No feature of Goetschius's theory met with more disapproval from American theorists than his definition of transient modulation. Soon after the appearance of his work in the United States, authors of harmony texts began to object to the notion that only two chords are required to replace an existing tonal center with a new one.

Goetschius had made the distinction between an altered chord and a modulation according to the single chord that follows the alteration. If the alteration is followed by a chord confirming the original key, the chord is nothing more than an altered harmony in the key. If the chord following the alteration is the tonic of the key suggested by the altered tone, however, a modulation is said to occur. Further, this modulation is said to be complete only if the new key is confirmed by subsequent harmonies (and preferably a cadence). The modulation is transient if the two chords are followed by chords clearly indicating the original key. Since the most direct means of modulation is through the dominant of the new key, the simplest and most common form of transient modulation consists of the dominant of a new key resolving to its tonic. In making such a definition, Goetschius had followed the tradition established by European theorists. Gottfried Weber, and later Ebenezer Prout, had handled the matter in just the same way. However, many American theorists were reluctant to accept the concept of transient modulation.

In *Harmony Simplified* Francis York distinguishes between ordinary altered chords and chromatic chords. A chromatic chord, according to York, is one whose alteration changes not only its shape but also its function in the key. "For example, if the ii7 is made II7, its character both as a minor chord and as a supertonic is lost. If it progresses to the V it produces the effect of a new key, and we say that it brings about a transition (modulation). If, however, it progresses to the I$_c$ or V7, either of these chords strongly contradicts any transitional tendency, and we call the chord chromatic."[130] Such a distinction is similar to the one Goetschius had made. York states: "Chromatic chords try to change the key but are not allowed to do so."[131]

Despite this distinction York is not convinced of Goetschius's notion of transient modulation:

> There is one class of progressions that seem to lie between transitions on the one hand and chromatic chords on the other. Any chord of a key (except vii°) may be preceded by a major chord (with or without a minor seventh) formed on the fifth above, and still no real transition produced. Thus the progression III, vi, if followed immediately by the proper progression of the vi, will give very little effect of transition. Such progressions are the same as passing transitions, only they are so very fleeting that the result is simply a strengthening of the original chord by giving it a quasi-tonic effect.[132]

York is at a loss for a method of symbolizing such a progression, however, and in his analysis of the passage in Figure 98 he shows each pair of chords as a modulation.

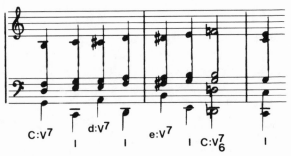

Figure 98.   Beethoven, Sonata, Op. 14, No. 2 (York, p. 88)

Frank Shepard approaches the problem by noting that some altered chords have a "peculiarly close relationship" to diatonic chords in the key. The relationship is that of a dominant to its tonic: "There is a Chord of the seventh closely related to every Major and Minor triad. Therefore it would not be strange to find, that these related chords are sometimes used, although they are not, strictly speaking, in the key."[133] He refuses to call them dominant chords, because they are not based on the fifth scale degree. He must therefore find another name for them, and does so:

> Notice that the chord marked * [in Figure 99] is not strictly in the key of C but is apparently like the Dominant seventh in the key of A. It does lead to the *chord* of A, and is in so far like the chord of the Dominant seventh in the key of A. Now let it be noticed that the chord marked * is *like* the chord of the Dominant seventh: but as there can be but one chord of the Dominant seventh in a key, we must adopt some other way of describing the relationship of this chord to the triad on A, and will call it the "Attendant" chord of A.[134]

Figure 99. (Shepard, p. 166)

He later extends the definition of attendant chords to include dominant ninth-chords, diminished seventh-chords, and augmented sixth-chords.[135]

Shepard's symbol for an attendant chord is the letter A in brackets. Its application may be seen in the analysis in Figure 100.

Figure 100. Mendelssohn, Spring Song (Shepard, p. 168)

A comparison of the methods by which York and Shepard deal with the problem of transient modulation reveals the two sides of the dilemma. A chord that takes the shape of a dominant and progresses as a dominant is perceived by the ear as bearing a dominant relationship to the chord to which it progresses. If it is regarded as a genuine dominant, however, the chord to which it progresses must be regarded as a tonic. All this adds up to a modulation to a new key, which is precisely the explanation theorists of the time are trying to escape, with good reason. On the other hand, as York rightly observes, a chord that is thus altered ceases to act as a supertonic, a mediant, a submediant, or whatever, and it takes on a distinctly dominant function. A theorist who routinely explains it as an altered chord risks failure to point out the dominant relationship between it and its chord of resolution. Shepard begins his description by remarking upon this dominant-tonic relationship. His term "attendant-chord," however, does not indicate this relationship specifically enough. Other types of altered chords may be said to "attend" the chords to which they progress without bearing such a distinctly dominant relationship to them. Shepard discovers this when he admits the augmented sixth-chord to the category of attendant-chords.

The problem is addressed by Benjamin Cutter in his *Harmonic Analysis*. Cutter is normally open-minded about analytical problems, and no more so than in the following passage:

In a piece in C major . . . we may find the dominant or diminished seventh of D minor, with its resolution, and this followed by C major chords. Some theorists contend that such a progression is a modulation; that any chord which has the intervals of a dominant seventh, and is properly resolved, is an undoubted dominant. Other theorists contend that a real modulation is made only when the modulatory process is confirmed by a stay in its evident key; that these seeming modulations are only intensifications of triads of the key other than the primary tonic, generally the subordinate triads, accomplished by the use of their seventh chords; and that these chords or progressions in question are only altered chords, or progressions in the primary key, and are to be so marked. They quote that most startling and familiar example—the end of the Lohengrin Prelude, by Wagner—which, while seemingly moving through, or, as they sometimes say, "touching upon" such and such keys, really gives the ear the impression of A major, wonderfully enriched, but A major, all the time; many of them conceding, however, that this is an extreme case. A third party of theorists, acknowledging the difficulties of the matter, hold that while this passage in question may be in A major, to mark the many chromatic harmonies as chromatic alterations in this key, is to strain the key unwarrantably; they would call each apparent change of key a real change, with a mental reservation as to the correctness of the analysis; would, perhaps, write two figurings, each one tenable, and depending upon the point of view.

In opposition to all this, the old-school men say that the modern ear has heard so many modulations that it has become blunted, dazed; that if the ear were fresher and keener, it would call each progression in question an undoubted change of tonality; and they refer their opponents back to the impressions of youth, when each chord change ravished the auditory nerve, and each seeming shift in the seat of the key, however fleeting, was felt as a genuine thing. They say, further, that the short and fleeting modulation, the Digression, so-called, is as much of the composer's stock in trade as that deliberate modulatory procedure in which the forces of the key are drawn up in array.

In this matter it is difficult to lay down a hard and fast rule. In many instances the analyst must use his own judgment, and the ear, which is plainly the last court of appeal, must be called upon to decide. And as ears do not always hear alike, the validity of more than one interpretation, based on the individual point of view, is evident.[136]

Cutter prefers to analyze the harmonies in question as altered chords. He refers to them as "apparent dominants," recommending they be analyzed when feasible in the original key.[137] He observes that the root progression of a fifth from an apparent dominant to its chord of resolution fits neatly into the natural scheme of harmonic progression by fifths. Rather than undermining the tonal center, then, an apparent dominant adds strength to the progression toward the ultimate tonic. "This feature of the thing leads many to say 'altered chords' where a man of the old school says 'modulation.'"[138]

In his analysis of the passage shown in Figure 101, Cutter analyzes the chord at a in C major, as a I_6 with a raised root, remarking, "Too short for a modulation." Of the chord at b, which he considers a dominant seventh with a raised root, still in C major, he says, "Some would call this A minor."[139] Of the passages in Figure 102 he observes, "The old-fashioned marking would read: d V7, G V7; and the G-sharp of the preceding measure would probably be called a passing tone. The impressions are certainly those of dominants, but whether apparent or real the listener must decide. We call them apparent dominants, and stay in C."[140]

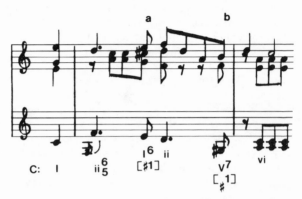

Figure 101.   Schumann, Op. 68 (Cutter, p. 113)

Figure 102.   Schumann, Op. 68 (Cutter, p. 115)

Cutter's analyses illustrate a notable disadvantage of the altered-chord explanation. By analyzing an apparent dominant simply as an altered chord, Cutter ascribes to it an undue degree of diatonic function. Whatever the chord at Figure 101*a* may be, it certainly is not a tonic triad in C, in any usual sense. Similarly, the chords marked vi7 and ii7 in Figure 102 have surrendered a great deal of their submediant and supertonic character by being altered into the shapes of dominant seventh-chords. Moreover, Cutter's analyses do not indicate the special dominant-tonic relationship that each of these chords bears to its chord resolution.

In *Modulation and Related Harmonic Questions* (1919), Arthur Foote concurs with Goetschius's opinion. Foote requires a genuine modulation to be followed by a confirmation of the new key, but he admits the possibility of transient modulation anyway:

> Theorists formerly held that every change of key . . . was to be considered a modulation, without regard to the length of the progression, and whatever its effect. A broader view is this—that one which is confirmed by a stay in the new key for a satisfactory length of time is to be regarded as definite and conclusive, but in cases such as those shown in [Figure 103], while the modulation may be made in the same manner as is the case with the former, changes of key succeed each other so rapidly as to justify a different classification, these being appropriately termed Transient Modulations.[141]

Figure 103.   Chopin, Nocturne, *Op. 9, No. 1 (Foote, p. 9)*

In instances such as the passage shown in Figure 104, in which each apparent dominant seventh resolves to another rooted a fifth below, Foote simply marks each seventh-chord V7 without specifying a key: "There is simply a succession of V7, that causes a rapidly shifting series of harmonies which carry us from C to A-flat, the result of such a series being always an inevitable modulation which is finally effected by the last V7."[142]

Donald Tweedy follows Goetschius's method even more closely than does Foote. Tweedy describes transient modulation using a fence gate as metaphor:

> Quite frequently, the gate of the fence is swung open as if we were to proceed into the territory of the new key; then, with our first step on

Figure 104. Chadwick, Scherzino, *Op. 9, No. 1 (Foote, p. 9)*

the other side of the fence, we change our minds, turn on our heel, and come right back. This is the type of modulation known as *transient.* Technically, it occurs when the chord of resolution in the new key is simultaneously an active chord in the old, pivoting us back immediately into the tonality from which we have just come.[143]

If, however, the "dominant" chord is not followed by its chord of resolution but by a chord in the original key, Tweedy analyzes it as an altered chord in the key: "Chords containing accidental notes may be named and symbolized precisely as if the accidentals were not there, provided the chord-succession reveals no modulations."[144] Tweedy, like Goetschius, distinguishes altered chords from modulation.

Tweedy's analysis of the last two phrases of the chorale "Valet Will Ich Dir Geben" illustrates his use of the concept of transient modulation. Although the four-measure excerpt begins and ends in E-flat major, he discovers modulations to A-flat major and F and C minor. The transient modulation to B-flat is bracketed because he considers the third chord from the end to be an altered supertonic seventh-chord in E-flat.[145] Even so, five modulations in four measures seem rather extravagant.

The notion that a listener can perceive so many changes of tonality in such a short duration strains credibility.

Figure 105.   Bach, Chorale "Valet Will Ich Dir Geben" (Tweedy, p. 28)

George Wedge objects to analyses which show such a dense concentration of modulation. He considers that a new tonal center requires a great deal of confirmation before it effectively supersedes the previous one; modulation is a procedure reserved for important structural purposes in a composition.[146] To Wedge the notion of several modulations in a few moments is unthinkable: "Psychologically this is most upsetting to the understanding of a composition. The ear accepts a given tonality and is not easily taken out of it. The ear certainly does not agree with the theorist who registers four modulations in the introduction to Beethoven's First Symphony or a modulation in the first phrase of Mendelssohn's Wedding March."[147]

Wedge's solution to the problem of transient modulation is similar to Shepard's. Wedge names the foreign chords in question "embellishing chords" and divides them into two types: dominant embellishments and diminished-seventh embellishments. The symbol for a dominant embellishment is X or X7 (to which figured-bass numerals may be appended to show inversions) and that for a diminished-seventh embellishment is 07.[148] The use of these symbols is illustrated in Figure 106.

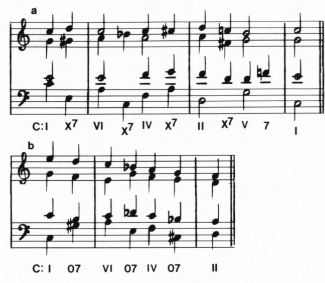

Figure 106. *Wedge, 2:1, 22*

As could be expected, Wedge's system suffers from the same lack of specificity as does Shepard's. The dominant relationships of Wedge's embellishing chords to the chords of their resolution are frequently obscure and sometimes nonexistent. The progressions in Figure 107*a* and *b* might be explained as deceptive resolutions; in *a* with a simultaneous change of mode, in *b* with a seventh added to the chord of resolution. (Wedge permits the parallel fifths in *b* because "the tones of the embellishing chords are unessential."[149]) However, the "dominant" embellishment in *c* cannot conceivably be a dominant of the chord to which Wedge resolves it. Similarly, the diminished-seventh embellishment at *d* does not bear the traditional vii°7–I relationship to what Wedge considers its chord of resolution.[150] Granted that embellishing chords are not necessarily intended to be dominants of the chords to which they resolve, Wedge's system is incapable of indicating the types of relationships they do bear to their resolutions.

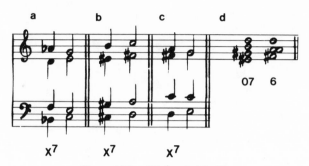

Figure 107. Wedge, 2:56, 22

Some theorists of the 1930s symbolize the progressions in question by showing the dominant-tonic relationship with the numerals V–I in parentheses. Such a system is used by Carleton Bullis in *Harmonic Forms* (1933). Bullis considers the progression of the foreign chord to its resolution to be borrowed from another key. To describe the foreign chord itself, Bullis uses Shepard's term "attendant chord."[151] Bullis's analysis of a borrowed progression is shown in Figure 108*a*.

A similar symbolization is used by William Mitchell in *Elementary Harmony* (1939). Mitchell borrows the term "applied dominant" from Heinrich Schenker and uses it to describe the foreign chord. His analysis shows the dominant relationship by means of the numerals V–I, $\frac{7}{V}$–I, or V^{7}_{II}–I in parentheses, preceded by the word "color," as shown in Figure 108*b*.[152]

The practice of showing the dominant-tonic relationship in parentheses beneath the regular analysis presents a solution to a serious defect of earlier systems. By specifying (V–I), the theorist is able to express the nature of the relationship between the two chords. The system is flexible enough to allow a theorist who wishes to treat leading-tone chords as independent harmonies to show this as (VII–I) in his analysis. The system may even be adapted to accommodate such nondominant relationships as (IV–I). By parenthesizing the V–I, the theorist minimizes the appearance of modulation.

It is interesting that the parenthesized symbols are so

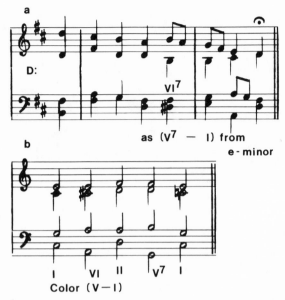

Figure 108. Luther, "A Mighty Fortress" (Bullis, p. 178); Mitchell, p. 190

convenient that they suit both Bullis and Mitchell, who differ over the derivation of these progressions. As previously noted, Bullis considers these progressions to be borrowed from another key. If the fifth chord of Figure 108a is borrowed from E minor, why analyze it as VI7 at all? To do so implies that it has a legitimate diatonic function in D major, which Bullis's explanation certainly does not seem to indicate. Mitchell regards the applied dominants as altered chords, which do not surrender their diatonic significance: "VI–II in a C major context will continue to operate as VI–II regardless of the applied color as long as the surrounding bass tones and chords assert that key."[153] To Mitchell, the dominant-tonic relationship is nothing more than a matter of "color."

It is perhaps too easy for a theorist working after 1938 to find fault with the explanations of Shepard, Cutter, Wedge, and others who reject the notion of transient modulation; they certainly deserve credit for recognizing the fallacy inherent in the concept and for attempting to replace it with a more accurate description of the phenomenon. European theorists whose works were appearing in the United States at the time were of no help in the matter; the treatises of Büssler and Rimsky-Korsakov, for instance, both make use of the transient-modulation explanation. The only European theorist who might have been of assistance was Heinrich Schenker, whose influence in the United States, however, was only beginning to be felt in the 1930s.

By comparing the weaknesses of the solutions proposed by the aforementioned theorists, it is possible to arrive at a set of requirements for a satisfactory explanation of the phenomenon. Such an explanation must present the enigmatic foreign "dominant" chord as a dependent of the chord to which it resolves; the foreign chord must not be represented simply as an altered chord performing a routine diatonic function in the key. Further, a satisfactory analysis should somehow express the dominant-tonic relationship—or whatever relationship—between the foreign chord and its chord of resolution, without stating or implying a change of tonality.

An explanation that meets these requirements is given by Walter Piston in *Principles of Harmonic Analysis* (1938): "Any degree of the scale, major or minor, (with the exception of the leading-tone, a purely melodic note) may be preceded by its dominant without disturbing the tonality. That is, a dominant seventh chord constructed on the first degree would be the dominant of the fourth degree and hence should be called V of IV."[154] Piston states that such a chord may take any of the forms of a normal dominant chord; that is, it may be a dominant seventh- or ninth-chord, may contain a raised fifth, or may appear without its root. It may even resolve deceptively; for instance, V of IV may resolve to IV's relative minor chord, II. In *Harmony* (1941) Piston uses the term "secondary dominants," which has since come into general use: "These temporary dominant chords have been referred to by theorists as attendant chords, parentheses chords, borrowed chords, etc. We shall call them secondary dominants, in the belief that the term is slightly more descriptive of their function."[155]

Of the solutions presented by American theorists, Piston's is the most feasible. His term "secondary dominant" is quite descriptive of the chord in question. The analysis "V of IV (or whatever)" is usually equally successful, especially when only a single secondary dominant appears before its triad of resolution. This method is less descriptive, however, when it is applied to deceptive resolutions of secondary dominants or to series of dominant seventh-chords, such as the one shown in Figure 109. The analysis in Figure 109 does not adequately show the dominant relationship of each secondary dominant to the next. It is necessary to know that the V of V substitutes for the II as a recipient of the resolution of the V7 of II. In any case, Piston's explanation of secondary dominants is clear enough, and his analysis usually effective enough, that the entire concept has since been absorbed into standard theoretical usage.

Bb: IV   V of VI V7of II V of V V7   I   II6   V7   I

Figure 109.   Mozart, Symphony No. 40, K.V. 550

4
An Age of Observation: 1939–1966

Walter Piston and His Influence

Underlying the many appearances and developments of individual ideas during the history of music theory, there has always been slower but nonetheless important movement in the philosophy of music theory. Since the beginnings of European theory in ancient Greece and the Middle Ages, two basic philosophies of theory have competed. The first holds theory to be the study of a system ordained by nature. According to this outlook the materials of music are dictated by such immutable laws as the mathematical division of a vibrating body or the naturally produced harmonic series. Opposing this is the philosophy that musical patterns are formed by human preference; that man, a creature of habit, reuses musical patterns that please him and that these patterns solidify into a system of rules, which then becomes codified as music theory.

Many of the basic tenets of Western harmonic theory arose from the acoustical speculation which began with Gioseffo Zarlino's *Institutione harmoniche* and which culminated in Jean Philippe Rameau's monumental discoveries. However, in the nineteenth century, following Rameau's work, acoustical speculation became so complicated that it was of little value to the practicing musician. But then Gottfried Weber renounced acoustics as a basis for music theory and substituted his observation of the practice of the composers of his time. The practical aspect of theory was revived by Weber and his followers and was introduced into the United States. But with the appearance of Alfred Day's theory in England the acoustical facet of theory began to regain significance. Its importance was further enlarged by Percy Goetschius, whose theory of harmonic progression depended upon an acoustically derived fifth.

The appearance of Walter Piston's *Harmony* in 1941 marks a return to the practical philosophy of theory. Like Gottfried Weber, Piston rejects acoustics and mathematics as the foundation of theory, instead basing his system on the observation of musical practice. Piston states that theory is "the collected and systematized deductions gathered by observing the practice of composers over a long time, and it attempts to set forth what is or has been their common practice. It tells not how music will be written in the future, but how music has been written in the past." Throughout the work Piston systematically rejects opportunities to support his statements with acoustical arguments. "Rules are announced as observations reported, without attempt at their justification on aesthetic grounds or as laws of nature."[1]

It can be justifiably argued that a theorist like Piston, by rejecting a mathematical or acoustical basis, deprives himself of an indispensable arbiter of theoretical questions. Prout, for instance, could state that the subdominant is really a part of the dominant and support that claim by referring to his acoustical theory. Goetschius could use his acoustical theory to show that the subdominant is actually derived from the supertonic. Musical practice can often provide valuable corroboration for such theories already derived. However, observation of a vast body of musical practice provides, of itself, no absolute answers to many theoretical questions. Musical practice cannot be cited to determine absolutely, for instance, whether the chord II is a substitute for the IV, or whether the IV is derived from II, or, again, whether VII is derived from V or is an independent harmony. On the other hand, theorists who work with a preconceived acoustical basis often appear to be bound by the procedures inherent in that basis. A reversion to an empirical philosophy seems to free theory from the restrictions of acoustical bases, allowing new ideas to appear, many of which are then accounted for in the next period of acoustical speculation. For Gottfried Weber, the observation of musical practice produced a sensible set of fundamental chord forms, a useful scheme of analytical symbols, and some important ideas regarding the function of chords. In Piston's case, it produces, among other things, an extension of ideas of harmonic function, a new view of chromatic harmony, and the concept of harmonic rhythm.

Born in Maine in 1894, Walter Piston first studied music with various private teachers in Boston. After World War I he entered Harvard University, where he graduated summa cum laude in 1924. He spent the next two years studying composition in Paris and upon his return to the United States, he was appointed to the faculty at Harvard University. He died in 1976. Piston is recognized as one of America's important composers, as well as a theorist and teacher. Besides his *Harmony*, his theoretical works include *Principles of Harmonic Analysis* (1938), *Counterpoint* (1947), and *Orchestration* (1955).

Piston has a notable advantage over Weber in that he is observing a fully developed harmonic system, which is no longer in general use by composers. The era during which this system is used is dubbed the period of "common practice," and Piston defines it thus: "Historically the period in which this common practice may be detected includes roughly the eighteenth and nineteenth centuries. During that time there is surprisingly little change in the harmonic materials used and in the manner of their use."[2] The scales used during this period are the major, the minor (harmonic and melodic), and the chromatic. Piston observes that the chromatic scale is generally treated as a variant of either the major or the minor scale. He considers the melodic minor scale to be a modification of the harmonic minor scale. Thus there are only two basic scale forms, major and harmonic minor.[3] It may be noted that Piston introduces the Roman numeral symbols in his exposition of the scale and uses them to denote individual scale degrees and the functions implied by these degrees.

Each scale degree and the triad built upon it (except the VII) are considered to represent either a tonal or a modal function. Tonal functions are those which define the tonic center; these include I, IV, and V: "Dominant and subdominant seem to give the impression of balanced support of the tonic, like two equidistant weights on either side of a fulcrum [see Figure 110]."[4] In addition to these functions, Piston mentions that the supertonic is "most often treated as the dominant of the dominant [see Figure 111a]. Harmonically, however, the supertonic often tends to become absorbed into the subdominant chord, especially in certain positions, and is sometimes spoken of as a substitute for the subdominant [see 111b]."[5] Piston concludes that the supertonic should also be considered a tonal degree, with the reservation that it has "much less tonal strength" than the other three tonal degrees. The mediant and submediant are modal degrees because they define the mode as either major or minor. The seventh degree is considered to be of melodic importance only, and Piston notes that the leading-tone triad is generally absorbed into the dominant.

I   V   I   IV   I

Figure 110.   Piston, p. 32

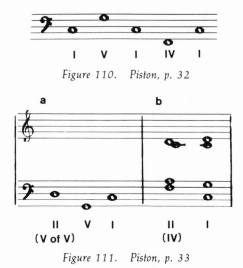

II   V   I   II   I
(V of V)   (IV)

Figure 111.   Piston, p. 33

Piston bases his exposition of harmonic progression solely on observation of the common practice of composers, "with no attempt to justify usage by suggesting reasons of an acoustical nature (although such physical hypotheses surely do exist)."[6] The results of Piston's observations are:

I is followed by IV or V, sometimes VI, less often II or III.
II is followed by V, sometimes VI, less often I, III, or IV.
III is followed by VI, sometimes IV, less often II or V.
IV is followed by V, sometimes I or II, less often III or VI.
V is followed by I, sometimes VI or IV, less often III or II.

VI is followed by II or V, sometimes III or IV, less often I.
VII is followed by III, sometimes I.[7]

It is notable that the most usual progression of each chord (except I and IV) in Piston's table is to the chord rooted a fifth below itself. Piston's observation thus confirms Rameau's and Goetschius's speculative theories. Piston points out that the dominant-tonic progression is the most satisfying, and observes that "other progressions with root moving down a fifth (or up a fourth) seem to have an analogous effect, although in less marked degree."[8] He notes that root movement up a fifth gives "the reverse effect" of that of the descending fifth. Piston also mentions root movements of seconds and thirds. He differentiates between the effects of ascending and descending third-progressions by noting that when the root progression moves up a third, "the root of the second chord has just been heard as the third of the first chord. On the other hand, when the root descends a third, the root of the second chord comes as a new note."[9]

In his discussion of inversions Piston presents an important concept of harmonic function. Chords without strong tonal connections seem to surrender their identity to more important tonal functions. For instance, Piston notes: "III6 is not usually an independent chord; it is a good example of the kind of chord made by temporary displacement of one or more tones of some other chord, in this case nearly always the dominant."[10] Similarly, the VI triad in first inversion is usually a tonic chord "with the sixth degree as a melodic tone resolving down to the fifth."[11] Examples of Piston's analyses are shown in Figure 112.

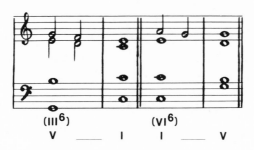

Figure 112.   Piston, pp. 51, 54

III6 and VI6 may also appear in weak rhythmic positions as passing chords. Similarly, VII6 is a passing chord when it appears in a rhythmically weak position between the tonic chord and its first inversion, as in Figure 113. Piston says that in this case it "may be analyzed as a grouping of melodic tones above the tonic root."[12]

I   VII6 I6   IV
(I ——————— IV)

Figure 113. Piston, p. 55

A similar phenomenon is observed by Piston in triads in the second inversion. Since he regards the fourth as a dissonant interval when it occurs upward from the bass, he considers the second inversion to be an unstable chord form, which is best explained as a configuration of nonharmonic tones.[13] He recognizes four categories of second-inversion chords. The cadential six-four chord, shown in Figure 114a, is the second-inversion tonic triad preceding the dominant chord of a cadence. He states that it is actually a dominant harmony with two appoggiatura, E and C, which resolve to the D and B of the V chord. A similar effect is seen at b, in which the appoggiatura six-four chord is used in a noncadential context in an accented position. The auxiliary six-four chord, shown at c, occurs in a weak rhythmic position and is actually formed by two auxiliary tones over the root of the prevailing harmony. The passing six-four, at d, is formed over a bass tone which is in the position of a passing tone. The other members of the chord are explainable as chord tones or auxiliary tones.[14]

Piston presents what has become the standard scheme of nearly related keys: any key has as its nearest relatives its dominant and subdominant keys and the relative minor or major keys of all three. What is striking about Piston's concept of key relation is his treatment of parallel modes. Two keys sharing a

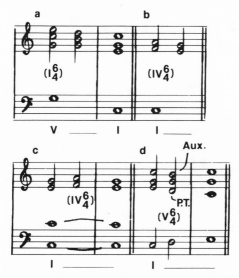

Figure 114. Piston, pp. 96, 102, 103

tonic, such as C major and C minor, have even a closer kinship than nearly related keys. "These keys are practically identical, having as they do the same tonal degrees and really differing only in the third degree." He observes that in common practice the two modes are often interchanged rather freely, as in the example in Figure 115, so that they are regarded "as simply two aspects of one tonality."[15] Such a fluctuation between modes is frequently used to enrich the harmonic color. Piston does not consider a simple change of mode to be a modulation, nor are chords from the parallel mode true altered chords.

Piston examines the mental processes involved in comprehending a modulation and concludes that modulation entails three stages: "First, a tonality has to be made clear to the hearer. Second, the composer at some point changes his tonal center. Third, the hearer is made aware of the change and the new tonal center is made clear to him."[16] He insists that every modulation involves a pivot chord, no matter how remote the new key might be: "Some modulations sound sudden and unexpected, and sometimes one feels that the composer did not intend an overlapping transition between the two keys. But there can be no modulation in which the last chord of the first key cannot be analyzed in terms of the second key, as a pivot

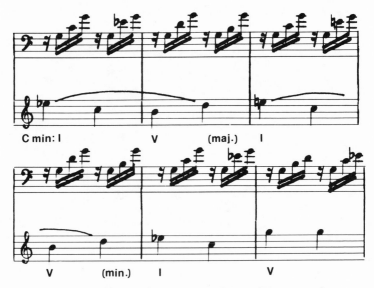

Figure 115.   Beethoven, Sonata, Op. 53 (Piston, p. 39)

chord."[17] In the example in Figure 116 the pivot chord, at the asterisk, is simultaneously I in B major (with the third taken from the parallel minor mode) and VI in D major. Following the pivot chord there must be a confirmation of the new key. He states that this confirmation is effected by a cadence in the new key.

Figure 116.   Beethoven, Symphony No. 9, Op. 125 (Piston, p. 148)

Piston's exposition of the dominant seventh-chord begins with an explanation of the chord's linear evolution: "The seventh, the factor which gives its name to the seventh chord, first appeared as a melodic non-harmonic tone. In the case of the seventh chord on the dominant, the seventh is often seen in this capacity [see Figure 117a]. The next evolutionary step was naturally the inclusion into the harmonic vocabulary of the vertical cross-section G–B–D–F as a chord, which we call V7 [see Figure 117b]."[18] Considered as a chord, the dominant seventh has two dissonant intervals, the seventh and the tritone, and each must resolve. Although Piston has not presented the theory of active and inactive scale degrees, he does regard the third and seventh of the V7 chord as "tendency tones." The third, the leading tone, must resolve upward to the tonic, and the seventh of the chord resolves downward, stepwise, to the third of the tonic triad.[19]

The dissonant seventh in any seventh-chord may be prepared in any of several ways: "The preparation or non-preparation of dissonance is a detail of style which may be expected to vary with different composers and which may be inconsistent in two works of different purpose by the same composer."[20] He considerably broadens the concept of preparation by including as one form a stepwise approach to dissonance. He categorizes preparation of dissonance in order of "perfection," as illustrated in Figure 118: "A dissonance is perfectly prepared when it enters as a suspension (a.). Next to that it may enter as a repeated tone (b.). It is prepared, although less perfectly, if it enters by step (c.). It is not prepared if it enters by skip (d.)."[21]

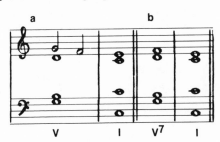

Figure 117. Piston, p. 151

Piston acknowledges the dominant ninth-chord, which may appear complete or without its root. Just as he considers the triad on the leading tone to be a dominant harmony, he refers to the leading-tone seventh-chord as V_9°. He

Figure 118.   Piston, p. 161

is reluctant to consider chords of the ninth on nondominant degrees to be independent chords; he observes that such a chord is usually the result of an appoggiatura or a suspension. Similarly, he is averse to the concept of independent eleventh- or thirteenth-chords in any position:

> In the following example [see Figure 119*a*], a thirteenth-chord is shown with all its factors, a sonority quite foreign to the period of harmonic common practice. It is also shown (*b.*) as it usually occurs. Playing of this second arrangement will demonstrate the high improbability of the missing thirds, especially A and C, and will also show the strong implication in the note E that it represents D, whether or not it actually resolves to it.[22]

Chords of the eleventh and thirteenth are thus actually results of appoggiature, suspensions, or pedal tones. In the case of an eleventh- or thirteenth-chord formed by an appoggiatura chord over a root, Piston's analysis shows the Roman numerals for both the appoggiatura chord and the root, separated by the virgule (/). An analysis of the chord as an eleventh- or thirteenth-chord may also be given, in parentheses.

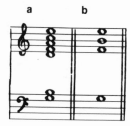

Figure 119.   Piston, p. 259

The concept of the secondary dominant has already been examined. It may be noted that Piston himself symbolizes secondary dominants using the preposition "of" (e.g., "V of IV") rather than the virgule ("V/IV"); he reserves the virgule for the purpose shown in Figure 120. Only later would theorists appropriate the virgule to symbolize secondary dominants.

Figure 120.   Beethoven, Sonata for Violin and Piano, Op. 30, no. 1 (Piston, p. 265)

A slight ambiguity in Piston's exposition of secondary dominants is brought about by his definition of them as dominants of scale degrees, rather than of triads: "Any *degree of the scale* may be preceded by its own dominant harmony without weakening the fundamental tonality."[23] Throughout the chapter he speaks of "the dominant of the second degree," "the dominant of the third degree," and so forth. This implies that the normal resolution of a secondary dominant is not restricted to the diatonic triad on the appropriate scale degree but may legitimately be to any good chord rooted on that degree. Implicit in other facets of Piston's explanation, however, is the notion that secondary dominants are, in fact, dominants of triads. For instance, he refers to the secondary dominant and its "tonic" as "a tonal unit of two chords." He does not admit a secondary dominant of VII, or of II in a minor key, since these triads are diminished and cannot act as temporary tonic chords. It is thus not entirely clear whether Piston intends secondary dominants to be dominants of scale degrees or of chords.

Piston does not consider secondary dominants to be altered chords. Chords resulting from the interchange of modes are also excluded as altered chords, since Piston regards the two parallel modes as a single tonality. The category of altered chords includes only the types shown in Figure 121: *a*, the diminished seventh-chords on the raised supertonic and raised submediant; *b*, the Neapolitan sixth-chord; *c*, the augmented sixth-chords; and *d*, the various augmented triads. He observes that the Neapolitan sixth-chord and the augmented sixth-chords originated in the inversions shown in Figure 121 and were only later recognized in other inversions. He therefore tolerates such expressions as "the Neapolitan sixth in root position."[24] He notes that the Neapolitan sixth is strongly subdominant in character and observes that it may appear either as an independent altered chord or as a result of a chromatic appoggiatura to the fifth of a subdominant triad, as in Figure 122.

Figure 121.   *Altered chords (Piston)*

Figure 122.   *Mozart, Quintet, K.V. 515 (Piston, p. 292)*

Piston states that the augmented sixth-chords are nondominant in function. He insists that the augmented sixth interval is formed by a subdominant with a raised root, rather than by a secondary dominant with a lowered fifth.[25] His illustration is shown in Figure 123. In presenting the augmented sixth-chords he expresses reluctance to adopt the labels "French," "Italian," and "German," which he says are not as universally accepted as the term "Neapolitan sixth."[26] He treats the two spellings shown in Figure 124 as two distinct chords: the IV $^{\sharp\,6}_{\;\,3}$, at *a*, is derived from the minor mode and precedes the dominant triad; the II $^{\sharp\,6}_{\;\,\;3}$, or chord of the doubly augmented fourth, precedes a cadential I $^{6}_{4}$ chord. Piston's reasoning is that D-sharp resolves upward to E, while E-flat tends downward to D.[27]

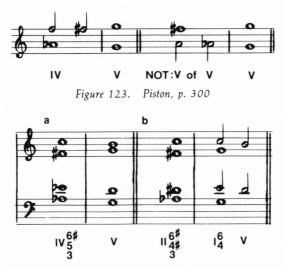

IV   V   NOT:V of V   V

Figure 123.   Piston, p. 300

IV$^{6\sharp}_{\;5}_{\;3}$ V   II$^{6\sharp}_{\;4\sharp}_{\;3}$ I$^{6}_{4}$ V

Figure 124.   Piston, pp. 302, 305

An important feature of Piston's work is his concept of harmonic rhythm. Other theorists had been conscious of the effects that harmony and rhythm have on each other; Goetschius, for instance, had been dealing with just this when he had proposed the harmonic suspension and harmonic anticipation. But Piston is the first theorist to attempt a systematic explanation of harmonic rhythm. His explanation forms a starting point from which other theorists can develop a more unified theory of harmonic rhythm.

Piston states that the harmonic rhythm of a passage of music may coincide with the melodic rhythm, as in Figure 125*a*, or it can operate independently of it, as at *b*.[28] He observes that certain harmonic progressions are conducive to either strong-to-weak or weak-to-strong rhythmic situations. A root progression of a fifth or second is a strong progression; that is, it has a rhythmic effect of weak-to-strong. A root progression of an ascending third has a weak (strong-to-weak) rhythmic effect, and that of a descending third has neither effect.[29] Piston hastens to add that these harmonic-rhythmic progressions are not absolute: "The fact is that any progression is capable of being sensed as down-up or up-down."[30] The possible interpretations are multiplied when more than two chords in succession are considered. The strong progression IV–V–I–V, for instance, is capable of any of the interpretations shown in Figure 126. Other factors must therefore be considered.

Figure 125. Beethoven, *Sonata, Op. 53 (Piston, p. 124); Sonata, Op. 31, no. 3 (Piston, p. 123)*

Figure 126.   Piston, p. 131

One important factor in harmonic rhythm is the agogic element: "Long and short values, it is generally agreed, are synonymous with heavy and light, strong and weak, rhythmic qualities." Another important factor in determining the harmonic-rhythmic value of a chord is the tempo of the passage. Of Figure 127, for instance, Piston says that "the speed of the music justifies a broader view of the harmony, so that the harmonic meter of one chord per measure seems reasonable. . . . On the other hand, in a slow tempo the passing chords are dwelt upon long enough to give them harmonic significance [Fig. 128]."[31] Another factor occasionally affecting harmonic rhythm is dynamic indication. In the example in Figure 129, for instance, the dominant chord at the end of the first measure might ordinarily be considered a passing chord, but the *sforzando* is enough emphasis to give it harmonic significance. Figure 129 is considered an exceptional case. Dynamic indications and accents usually serve to confirm the natural rhythmic effect, rather than to contradict it.

Piston's concept of strong and weak rhythmic values emerges in his presentation of nonharmonic tones: "All non-harmonic tones are rhythmically weak, with the single exception of the appoggiatura."[32] To Piston, any tone that is attacked at a

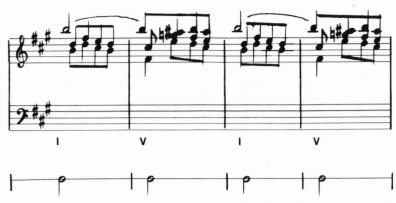

Figure 127.   Scarlatti, Sonata (Piston, p. 132)

Figure 128.   Haydn, Sonata (Piston, p. 133)

Figure 129.   Beethoven, Sonata, Op. 31, no. 3 (Piston, p. 132)

strong rhythmic moment is an appoggiatura, regardless of how it is approached. The examples in Figure 130, which other theorists might consider to be a suspension and a passing tone, are both analyzed by Piston as appoggiature.[33] Although his concept of the appoggiatura as a rhythmically accented, nonharmonic tone agrees with the definitions given by Robinson and Tweedy, Piston does not follow these two theorists by classifying the suspension as a type of appoggiatura. His distinction between the suspension and the appoggiatura approached from a unison rests on the matter of articulation. Referring to Figure 131, Piston explains the difference in rhythmic effect thus: "It is interesting to note [at *a*] that the melodic rhythm of the voice containing the suspension is strong-to-weak, long-to-short, while the harmonic rhythm is here felt as weak-to-strong. If the C were not tied over [as at *b*] the effect would be of an appoggiatura and the melodic rhythm would then agree with the harmonic rhythm."[34]

Figure 130. Haydn, Sonata; Brahms, Piano Concerto, Opus 83 (Piston, p. 86)

Other nonharmonic types presented by Piston are the passing and auxiliary tones, the anticipation, the *échappée* (or escape tone), and the *cambiata*. Piston is the first American

Figure 131. Piston, p. 87

theorist to consider the échappée an independent type of nonharmonic tone; previously it had been explained either as an irregular changing tone (Prout, Chadwick, Tweedy) or as an irregularly resolved anticipation (Goetschius, Cutter).

Of the original features of Piston's theory, the one most quickly absorbed into standard theoretical usage was the concept of the secondary dominant. It has been seen that previous American theorists had struggled to find an explanation of this phenomenon; the two extreme results, the "altered-chord" theory and the notion of transient modulation, were both unsatisfactory. Piston's secondary-dominant concept was seen as a valuable solution to an awkward theoretical problem, and most American writers were eager to accept it.

The absorption of the secondary-dominant concept is evident as early as 1943, in Paul Hindemith's *Traditional Harmony*.[35] Hindemith, who was teaching at Yale University at the time, appears to be the first theorist to borrow this idea from Piston.

Roger Sessions, in *Harmonic Practice* (1951), regards the secondary dominant as one means of accomplishing the "tonicization" of a nontonic chord (he borrows the idea of "tonicization" from Heinrich Schenker, whose influence will be examined later). Sessions, unlike Piston, considers VII to be an independent chord rather than an incomplete V7, and he accordingly makes a distinction between a secondary dominant and a secondary leading-tone chord. Sessions finds that the most frequently used form of the secondary leading-tone seventh is its fully diminished form, which is derived from the minor key but may resolve to either a major or a minor chord.[36]

He further extends the secondary-chord concept to include "relationships other than those of the dominant and the leading tone."[37] Thus it is possible to express a nondominant secondary function such as the II6 of IV in Figure 132. He also mentions the possibility of a secondary chord appearing after its normal chord of resolution; in such cases the secondary dominant relationship must be understood retrospectively. In the example in Figure 133, the chord at the *fermata* may be comprehended as the dominant of the III, which has already been sounded.

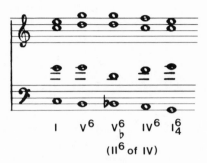

$$I \quad V^6 \quad V^6_\flat \quad IV^6 \quad I^6_4$$

$$(II^6 \text{ of } IV)$$

Figure 132. Sessions, p. 245

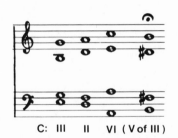

$$C: III \quad II \quad VI \ (V \text{ of } III)$$

Figure 133. Sessions, p. 247

A modification in the symbolism for secondary diminished seventh-chords may be found in *Materials and Structure of Music* (1966) by William Christ and others of Indiana University. The Indiana theorists eliminate the numeral VII from the symbol and show only the "diminished" sign ° and any necessary figured-bass numerals above the virgule. Thus, the chord F-sharp–A–C–E-flat in C major is shown simply as °7/V. By eliminating the VII from the symbol, they show the chord simply as a diminished seventh rooted on a neighboring tone, rather than emphasizing the leading-tone aspect of the root. Such an analysis has the advantage of bypassing potential confusion when the diminished seventh-chord is spelled enharmonically. To describe the chord the authors borrow Wedge's terminology, the "embellishing diminished seventh."[38]

The greatest difficulty in the secondary-dominant concept occurs when a series of secondary dominants is used, with each dominant resolving to the next, as in Figure 134. Here the analysis may appear misleading; a reader, in order to understand why V of II does not properly resolve to its "tonic" II, must realize that V of V is a substitute recipient for II of the resolution of V of II.

Bb: IV   V of VI   V⁷of II   V of V   V⁷   I   II⁶   V⁷   I

Figure 134.   Mozart, Symphony No. 40, K.V. 550

An attempt to solve this problem occurs in Wallace Berry's *Form in Music* (1966). He presents the possibility of a tertiary dominant, or, as he describes it, "a secondary dominant twice removed." He represents it by compounding the numeral-and-virgule symbol; for instance, V/V/V, says Berry, "would . . . describe the function of the A major triad in C major, when that triad functions as a dominant to the D major triad, which is V/V."[39]

This idea, in fact, had been presented by Piston himself four years earlier in the third edition (1962) of *Harmony*. In a chapter entitled "Extensions of Tonality," he analyzes the chord at the asterisk in Figure 135 thus: "The last chord in the second measure from the end, F minor, is obviously here II of IV rather than V of B-flat, so that its dominant before it has been given the somewhat awkward but nonetheless accurate description as V of II of IV."[40]

With the introduction of the secondary-dominant concept, a clearer notion of the requirements for a genuine modulation is possible. Sessions, for instance, requires that the pivot chord of a modulation be followed by "a point of decisive contact with the new key, which must then be clearly established by means of a cadence or its equivalent."[41] Other theorists since

Figure 135.   *Piston,* Harmony, *3rd ed., p. 331*

1941 have also generally considered the establishment of the new key to be an essential feature of a modulation.

According to Piston, the seventh-chord is the result of a melodic factor, namely, the seventh, which has been gradually absorbed into the harmony through tradition. This explanation of the seventh-chord is found in most theory texts since 1941. Even Allen McHose, by no means a Piston adherent, gives an exposition of the linear "development" of the seventh-chord.[42]

Sessions extends the concept that melodic factors may be absorbed into a chord through usage. His term for a nonharmonic tone is "accessory tone," which he says is responsible for any dissonant combination. In a seventh-chord, the seventh is really an accessory tone, which through usage has been "frozen" onto the triad; the triad thus loses its stable character. He does not adopt Piston's definition of "preparation," but he does say that the seventh may be prepared (in the sense that a suspension is prepared) or unprepared (approached by step or occasionally by skip).[43]

Sessions develops the concept of "frozen accessory tones" to include other combinations. The chords of the ninth, eleventh, and thirteenth are all thus explained. These, however, are not "frozen" to the extent that the seventh is, largely because the ninth, eleventh, and thirteenth are all capable of resolving downward, stepwise, to chord tones. "As a result of this fact, it is clear that while the seventh of the chord must in general be held until the resolution takes place, the ninth may be dropped [as in Figure 136] . . . without any serious loss of dissonant effect." He also explains that the first-inversion II7 chord—Rameau's "chord of the added sixth"—is indeed a IV triad with a tone a sixth above the bass. This sixth is "frozen" into the harmony.[44]

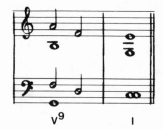

Figure 136.   Sessions, p. 225

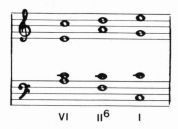

Figure 137.   Sessions, p. 229

Piston's concept of the interchangeability of the major and minor modes is also reflected in Sessions's work. Sessions considers the practice of "borrowing" from the opposite mode to be a means by which a composer may greatly extend the resources of tonality. Although either mode may borrow from the other, the most common modal alterations are those in which features of the major mode appear in the minor. He considers the Aeolian minor to be the basic form of the minor scale; when a raised sixth or seventh degree is used, as in the dominant harmony, this raised degree has been borrowed from the parallel major.[45] The authors of *Chromatic Harmony* (1965), Justine Shir-Clif, Stephen Jay, and Donald J. Rauscher, advance the theory that only the major mode may borrow features from the minor.[46]

The concept of a theory of harmonic rhythm has developed only gradually. The subject has not yet been adequately systematized, but is still in a formative stage. Sessions devotes a section to harmonic rhythm. He makes a commendable effort to systematize it by dividing the topic into two elements: rate of harmonic movement, and accent. Harmonic movement may involve rapid changes of harmony, in which case more energy is generated, or slower changes, in which case a more relaxed effect is achieved. He also mentions the rhythmic patterns that are created by harmonic movement, noting: "Once a pattern of harmonic movement or harmonic change has been established, the ear will be disappointed if the pattern is weakened."[47] He considers three types of accents to be involved in harmonic rhythm: accent of weight, accent of meter, and expressive accent. Accent of weight is exemplified by the arrival of the cadence of a musical phrase. Metric accent simply corresponds to the first beat of a measure. Expressive accentuation is caused by melodic or rhythmic contour; a melodic tone that is the highest point of the phrase, for instance, creates an expressive accent. An agogic accent is considered expressive.[48]

Christ, DeLone, Kliewer, Rowell, and Thompson devote a section of their work to the topic of harmonic rhythm. The Indiana theorists discuss the various effects of rapid and slow harmonic changes. They also mention the rhythmic patterns which can be created by harmonic changes. The Indiana theorists consider such a rhythmic pattern to be a resource a composer can draw on to create interest.[49] They note the role of the pedal point as a "camouflage" of the harmonic rhythm created by the upper voices.[50]

The philosophy of observation which Piston had proclaimed has largely been followed by subsequent writers. The value of an acoustical basis of a presentation of theory has considerably diminished since 1941. Sessions, for instance, writes: "The overtone series has been used to 'prove' many differing theories and to reinforce many differing sets of values. These proofs and evaluations, however, cannot be derived from the overtone series; they must instead be sought in terms of the various types of satisfaction which the ear—i.e., the musical imagination—demands and receives from music."[51] Interestingly, Sessions does not subscribe to Piston's concept of a period of "common practice," but instead prefers to recognize the continuing change in harmonic usage throughout the eighteenth and nineteenth centuries.[52]

An excellent illustration of a theory constructed upon the observation of a feature of musical practice is found in Richard Franko Goldman's *Harmony in Western Music* (1965). Using the perfect fifth as his basis, Goldman presents as the normal pattern the now-familiar progression of root movements of descending fifths toward the tonic. Goldman derives this fifth-progression from analogy with the cadence V–I. However, he states explicitly that the descending fifth of the progression V–I is not a result of nature or the harmonic series, but an accepted cliché of Western music: "the force of the dominant, that is, our sense that it requires resolution or movement towards a tonic, is arbitrary. It rests on no law of acoustics, but is an acquired meaning."[53] He supports his point by noting that other cultures have had other musical patterns which they have recognized as signal musical elements simply through repeated hearing. For instance, the "Landini" cadence had an especially forceful meaning in the fourteenth century to Europeans only because they had come to recognize it as a closing formula.[54]

    With the decline of the importance of acoustical theory, diagrams and explanations of the harmonic series have receded to less important positions in theory texts. When the acoustically derived major triad or perfect fifth is mentioned at all, it is only as an incidental feature accompanying a description of the harmonic practice of composers. Such a decline in acoustical theory would obviously have a drastic effect on the older Goetschius tradition, which would need to replace its acoustical basis with something else in order to survive.

Continuation of the Goetschius Tradition: Allen McHose

    It would be impossible for a complete systematic version of Goetschius's harmonic theory, with its original acoustical basis, to continue to develop in the 1940s as it had under Tweedy and Wedge. Piston's *Harmony* had marked a reversal of philosophy: the concept of an acoustical basis had given way to the procedure of deriving theory solely from the observation of musical practice. No longer would it be usual for a theory text to begin with a demonstration of the harmonic series, to which the theorist could refer constantly during his presentation. The "common practice" of composers had replaced the harmonic series as the basis of harmonic theory.

    If the Goetschius tradition were to continue at all, its acoustical basis would have to be replaced with something more sympathetic to the new philosophy. The new foundation would have to be capable of supplying concrete proof, especially proof of the theory of harmonic progression, as the old acoustical basis had done. The observation of practice, as Piston had presented it, would not be sufficiently absolute. However, observation can be systematized into a precise tabulation of the frequency of the appearance of certain musical patterns, a translation of these tabulations into percentages, and a formulation of theoretical conclusions based on these percentages—in other words, a statistical basis of theory.

Such a statistical basis is found in the work of Allen Irvine McHose, of the Eastman School of Music. McHose's *The Contrapuntal Harmonic Technique of the 18th Century* (1947) presents an exposition of harmonic theory based on extensive analysis of music of the late Baroque era, with special emphasis on the chorales of Johann Sebastian Bach. "During this period, the technical elements of the seventeenth century were evaluated and combined into a type of composition based on the principle of chord progression. This principle of chord progression establish-ed the concept of the key center."[55] McHose notes that Bach, Handel, and Carl Heinrich Graun, the composers he is observing, were contemporaries of Rameau, the originator of the theory of harmonic progression. McHose recognizes that stylistic changes affect the harmonic usage of the Classical and Romantic periods; he regards his study of early eighteenth-century practice as a norm, "from which comparative studies with other periods may readily be achieved."[56]

Although his study is based on analysis of complete compositions, he does not list these works specifically. Also somewhat disconcerting is that he studies differing bodies of music to arrive at various statistics. Whereas he uses the study of over two hundred Bach chorales to illustrate one point, he refers to a study of all 371 chorales for statistics to demonstrate suspensions, or of unspecified works of "Bach, Graun, Handel, and other contemporaries" to illustrate root movement.

McHose begins his exposition by explaining the triad and the theory of inversion, acknowledging Rameau for the latter. He illustrates Rameau's method of analysis by presenting the Bach chorale shown in Figure 138, with the notes of the fundamental bass beneath it. McHose assesses the frequency of the appearance of the intervals between each two fundamental bass notes and arrives at his figures:

> Considering the interval of the fourth as the inversion of the fifth, the intervals appear in the fundamental bass of the preceding example in the following frequency:
>
> | | |
> |---|---|
> | Prime | 6 |
> | Fifth apart | 26 |
> | Second apart | 2 |
> | Third apart | 4 |

That is, there were six repetitions of the same chord, twenty-six progressions with the roots of the chords a fifth apart, two progressions with the roots of the chords a second apart, and four progressions with the roots of the chords a third apart.[57]

Figure 138. Bach, Chorale "Was Gott tut, das ist wohlgetan" (McHose, p. 3)

McHose then performs a similar analysis on a Graun chorale and
discovers that it contains a greater frequency of root movement
by seconds. From analyses of additional works of the period,
McHose arrives at the following figures regarding root movement:

Prime	16%
Fifth apart	52%
Second apart	21%
Third apart	11%.[58]

        Since root progressions by fifths are clearly in the
majority, McHose concludes that the major key is defined by
arranging three major triads so that their roots are a fifth apart,

as in Figure 139; the central triad is the tonic. The minor key is established by three minor triads similarly arranged. The tones of the three principal triads of a key are arranged in linear fashion to form the scale, just as Rameau had done.

Figure 139. McHose, p. 4

At this point McHose indicates that he is parting company with Rameau's procedure. McHose's statement characterizes the "observation" philosophy of the time: "The error that Rameau and many theorists following him made was to become involved in mathematical and acoustical explanations to prove this theory of the key center. . . . What should have been done was to continue the analysis of the music."[59] In fact, Rameau had not used such an analysis of the music of his contemporaries as his starting point at all, but had obtained the interval of the fifth directly from his acoustical and mathematical bases.

McHose proceeds to study a number of Bach's chorales in search of a usual pattern of harmonic movement. He first examines chords used to approach the tonic. He outlines his procedure in this way: "1. The tonic chords were located. 2. The interval relation of the root of the preceding chord to the root of the tonic was tabulated. 3. The following was the result of the study [considering only the roots of the most frequent pretonic chords]."[60] The most common pretonic chords are the chords rooted on the dominant and the leading tone. McHose calls them chords of the "first classification."

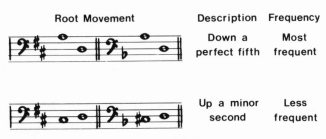

Root Movement		Description	Frequency
		Down a perfect fifth	Most frequent
		Up a minor second	Less frequent

Figure 140.   McHose, p. 6

McHose discovers that the two first-classification chords are usually preceded by chords rooted on the subdominant or supertonic. These accordingly become "second-classification" chords. The second-classification chords are, in turn, usually preceded by submediant chords or dissonant chords on the tonic; these form the third classification. The fourth classification contains only the triad on the mediant. Consolidating his results, McHose presents the table of normal chord progression shown in Figure 141.

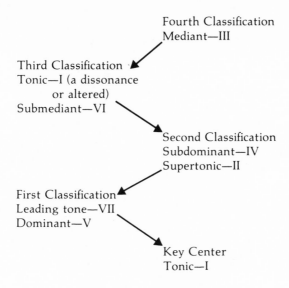

Fourth Classification
Mediant—III

Third Classification
Tonic—I (a dissonance
    or altered)
Submediant—VI

Second Classification
Subdominant—IV
Supertonic—II

First Classification
Leading tone—VII
Dominant—V

Key Center
Tonic—I

Figure 141. McHose, p. 9

McHose's scheme of chord progression as it is presented above differs from Goetschius's only slightly. McHose does not admit the VI triad to the tonic classification of harmony, as Goetschius had. Also, McHose regards the leading-tone triad in the first classification as an independent chord, rather than a derivative of the dominant, and he does not attempt to place the triad III in the first classification as a possible substitute for the V, as had Goetschius. In other respects, however, McHose's scheme of harmonic movement from an empirical basis from tabulations of the progressions used in Bach's chorales bears a close resemblance to Goetschius's scheme from an acoustical basis.

McHose adds to his theory two possibilities regarding the tonic: "1. The tonic chord may progress to any chord in its key. 2. The tonic chord may be used between two chords which form a normal progression without disturbing their classification."[61] The second had not occurred to Goetschius.

McHose reports that in music of the eighteenth century about 76 percent of root movement follows the normal progression. The remaining 24 percent is of three types: repetition, elision, and retrogression.[62] His regard of chord repetition is curious; one does not normally consider the repetition of a chord to constitute harmonic movement. The subject of chord repetition does give McHose the opportunity to observe: "The functions which are repeated most often are, first, tonic; second, dominant; third, subdominant; and fourth, supertonic."[63] This interesting observation is relevant to his scheme of progression; the closer a chord lies to the tonic center, the more apt it is to be emphasized by repetition. Elision and retrogression occur much less frequently than chord repetition. The most frequent elisions of classifications occur in the chord movements III–IV, VI–V, and IV–I. The most common retrogressions are VI–III, V–II, and V–IV. McHose notes that in the two examples that he presents the retrogressions are immediately followed by reversion to normal movement.

In the scheme of normal progression in the minor key, McHose includes triads formed by both the raised and lowered sixth and seventh scale degrees, noting the less frequently used forms. Thus, the tonic triad is usually minor, less often major; the dominant is usually major, less often minor, and so forth.[64] He considers both forms of the minor scale to be legitimate forms (though not equally frequent).

McHose recognizes both common-chord and chromatic modulation as types of modulation that may occur within a phrase. As a third type he introduces modulation that is made at the beginning of a phrase. Describing the modulation shown in Figure 142, he states, "Bach certainly considered the A-minor triad [beginning the second phrase] in its relation to the C center, rather than carrying A minor into the second phrase."[65] Perhaps so, but listeners will not recognize C major until they have heard the second and possibly the third chords of the second phrase.

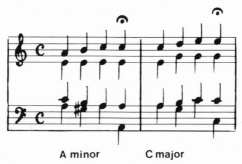

A minor   C major

Figure 142.   Bach, Chorale "Ach, wie nichtig" (McHose, p. 17)

McHose's exposition of altered chords is indebted to
Goetschius. An altered chord, says McHose, "must retain the
function of the basic diatonic chord from which it is derived."[66]
He lists the possible altered chords according to their classification. The only altered chords in the minor mode to be used by
Bach are those in the second classification. Besides the raised
sixth degree (which is considered a part of the minor key), the
only possible alterations in minor are the lowered second-scale
degree and the raised fourth.[67] The major mode admits of
alterations in every classification except the tonic. In his
analytical symbols he solves a long-standing problem of
Goetschius's symbols for altered chords by placing beneath the
sharp or flat in the analysis the appropriate scale-degree number.
For example, $\flat^{\mathrm{IV}\,7}$ represents a subdominant seventh-chord with
the third scale degree (*not* the chord third) flattened.

McHose recognizes eight types of nonharmonic
tones: the passing tone, the suspension, the neighboring tone,
the anticipation, the escape tone, the appoggiatura, the changing
tone, and the pedal point. Nonharmonic tones are classified
according to the manner in which they enter and resolve.
Although he does not introduce any new concepts regarding
nonharmonic tones, he does provide such fascinating statistics
as, "an analysis of the 371 chorales reveals that Bach used 1,661
suspensions of various types"; and "In a study of 200 chorales,
109 chains of single suspensions were found. Ninety-three were
groups of two suspensions, 13 were groups of three suspensions, one contained four suspensions, and two contained five
suspensions."[68] Such figures do not appear to affect McHose's

theory of nonharmonic tones, although they may be valuable material for a study of Bach's style

McHose's *Basic Principles of the Technique of 18th and 19th Century Composition* appeared in 1951, four years after *The Contrapuntal Harmonic Technique*. Although the harmonic theory in *Basic Principles* is generally the same as that in *Contrapuntal Harmonic Technique*, McHose elaborates on several points.

In *Basic Principles* his observation is not limited to the technique in Bach chorales. He still derives most of his statistics from late Baroque practice, but he also uses examples from the works of Mozart, Beethoven, Mendelssohn, Chopin, and other Classical and Romantic composers. However, if McHose is aware of differences in harmonic usage between one period and the next, he does not mention them.

Basic Principles opens with a chapter on acoustics, which would be an anachronism if it were to serve as the basis of McHose's theory. Its purpose, however, is simply to describe the physics of a musical sound. Frequency of vibrations is used briefly as a concept to define the proportions of consonant intervals in just intonation. McHose hastens to add that, with the exception of the octave, the intervals formed by equal temperament differ from those of just intonation by a few beats, a difference which musicians can accept.[69]

Rameau's derivation of the scale from the tonic, dominant, and subdominant triads is also presented. McHose lays particular emphasis on the harmonic origin of the scale and key. After quoting Sir Hubert Parry, McHose makes a statement which appears to be directed at Goetschius's theory of the origin of the scale:

> Even today there remain presentations of elementary theory which teach that the major and minor keys are established by the use of the major and minor scales. Some of these methods grossly misrepresent the entire concept of key feeling by making a minor key subservient to a major key. With this in mind, the author wishes to emphasize the theories of Rameau and subsequent theoretical scholars who stress the fact that the music of the 18th and 19th centuries is based on the characteristics of the fundamental bass progressions and that major and minor scales result from the types of chords erected on these fundamental bass tones.[70]

In support of the theory of the scale's origin in the three primary triads, McHose includes an appendix in which he explains the mathematical proportions of chords and scales in just intonation.

McHose elaborates upon the formation of the minor key. He first presents the natural minor by placing minor triads in the three principal positions. However, he observes that in Bach's usage the dominant of the minor key is generally a major chord, the subdominant is sometimes made major to accommodate an ascending sixth scale degree, and the tonic triad often appears as a major triad at the end of a composition in a minor key.[71] The complete harmonic and melodic content of a minor key, then, includes, not seven, but ten different tones, as illustrated in Figure 143; and major as well as minor triads are possible on the tonic, dominant, and subdominant. If major triads are permitted in all three positions of the tonality, what is the difference between major and minor? McHose addresses this question by citing the frequency of major and minor triads in each position in the works of Bach and his contemporaries. He finds that in the minor key minor triads on the tonic and subdominant are "very frequent," and a major triad on the dominant is likewise "very frequent."[72] These form the harmonic minor scale. Perhaps the most interesting aspect of McHose's presentation of the harmonic minor scale is the absence of any purely theoretical notions, such as the convenient explanation that the seventh scale degree is sharpened to improve its tendency as a leading tone. Rather, McHose remains loyal to his procedure and deduces the scale entirely from the systematic observation of the harmonic usage of the late Baroque.

Although McHose had recognized all types of diatonic seventh-chords in *Contrapuntal Harmonic Technique*, in *Basic Principles*

Figure 143. McHose, p. 107

he treats only the dominant seventh-chord, or "major-minor seventh," as he names it. He permits the seventh to enter in the manner of a suspension, passing tone, upper neighboring tone, or appoggiatura. He does not subscribe to the concept of secondary dominants (he regards these simply as altered chords), and therefore warns: "The major minor seventh chord appears in other classifications as an altered chord. For this reason, the author urges one to guard against the familiar and thoughtless nickname which is used, namely, dominant-seventh type or five-seven type."[73]

The Influence of Heinrich Schenker: William Mitchell, Allen Forte

The system of theory formulated by Henrich Schenker has stirred a great deal of interest and controversy among theorists in the United States. His theory has created serious interest in the structural analysis of music and has also influenced American works dealing with the purely harmonic aspect of theory.

Schenker was born in Poland in 1867. He studied composition with Anton Bruckner at Vienna but soon gave up composing to devote himself to theoretical analysis. He did not affiliate himself with any university or conservatory but privately taught theory and analysis until his death in 1935.

Schenker's first important work, *Harmonielehre*,[74] was published in 1906 as the first volume of his series "Neue Musikalische Theorien und Phantasien." In it certain of his unique theoretical ideas may be seen in their earliest forms. Schenker's acoustical basis in his *Harmonielehre* is remarkably similar to that of Goetschius; the perfect fifth, the most important natural relationship between two tones, is used to project a series of triad roots up from the tonic to include the roots of triads V, II, VI, III, and VII. The natural progression of these triads, however, is in descending, not ascending, fifths toward the tonal center. The motion of descending fifths is due to an "artistic inversion" of the natural upward direction. By such "artistic inversion," the subdominant, a fifth below the tonic, is determined. The tones F-sharp, C-sharp, G-sharp, and D-sharp in the triads in Figure 144 conflict with the F, C, G, and D, which are more nearly related by fifths to the tonal center. Therefore, the sharpened tones are replaced by the natural tones with which they conflict, and the diatonic triads of C major are thus formed. Schenker notes that the fifth from F to B in the fifth-progression I–IV–VII–III–VI–II–V–I is a diminished fifth. The purpose of this diminished fifth, he says, is to arrest the downward fifth motion I–IV and rechannel it so that it once again approaches the tonic.[75]

Figure 144.   Schenker, Harmony, p. 39

Schenker regards the minor mode as an artificial construction, devised for artistic contrast with the major.[76]

Schenker's scheme of harmonic progression leads him to distinguish between actual harmonies in a progression and chords that are accidentally formed by linear activity. For instance, the combination at the asterisk in Figure 145, ordinarily a V chord in F-sharp minor, is not considered a functional chord because it occurs after the VI, not the usual position for a dominant harmony. The chord is thus merely a passing chord, formed accidentally by linear activity.[77] The passing-chord concept is, of course, one that had been made familiar by Richter's *Harmonielehre*. What is new is Schenker's use of his law of harmonic progression to detect passing chords.

Figure 145.   Bach, "St. Matthew Passion" (Schenker, Harmony, p. 144)

Schenker explains the seventh-chord as a combination of two chords (e.g., C–E–G and E–G–B form the chord C–E–G–B), an explanation he would later abandon.[78] He does consider the ninth-chord to be caused by passing motion of voices or pedal point.[79] For similar reasons he does not consider eleventh- or thirteenth-chords independent harmonies.

An important concept in the *Harmonielehre* is that of tonicization, or the strengthening of a nontonic harmony by temporarily treating it as a tonic. Schenker gives the example in Figure 146, in which the IV chord in the second measure is treated as a I in B-flat by the insertion of the E-flat in place of the expected E in the melody. Nonetheless, the effect is so temporary that to consider a modulation to B-flat would make no sense at all. Tonicization is also affected by the use of chords preceding the tonicized chord. The most usual example is that in which the tonicized chord is preceded by its own dominant—in modern terms, a secondary dominant.[80]

Figure 146.   Bach, Italian Concerto (Schenker, Harmony, p. 256)

After the publication of *Harmonielehre*, Schenker published a series of pamphlets entitled *Der Tonwille* (1926–29), in which he began to develop his graphic analysis to show structural harmonic motion. In *Der Freie Satz* (1935) Schenker presented the system of structural analysis for which he has since become known.

The basis of Schenker's mature theory is the concept that any composition is an elaborated projection of the tonic chord. The movement of the harmony throughout the composition is toward less stable areas, notably the dominant, and finally back to the tonic. This entire movement is represented by the

Ursatz, the fundamental bass progression I–V–I. The *Ursatz* may also include a structural chord preceding the dominant, either II, IV, or III.[81]

The *Ursatz* forms the basis for the *Hintergrund*, the most general analysis of the entire work. The next level (or levels) of detail, called the *Mittelgrund*, shows the *Ursatz* elaborated by the more important structural harmonic events of the work. The *Vordergrund*, the last level, shows the harmonic events of the work in considerable detail. By this type of analysis, any chord in the composition may be assessed for its significance and function in relation to the *Ursatz* chords.

In addition to harmonic motion, Schenker's system shows general melodic movement. The *Ursatz* includes not only the fundamental bass progression but also a general outline of the melody, beginning on scale degree 3, 5, or 8 (another manifestation of the projection of the tonic harmony through the work) and progressing toward the tonic degree 1.[82] This progression, like the harmonic motion, is shown in more and more detail as the analysis passes from the *Hintergrund* through the *Mittelgrund* to the *Vordergrund*.

Schenker's theory has been discovered only gradually by American theorists, notably due to the lack of translations of his works. Information on his theory of structural analysis has been limited in America to the works of a few informed proponents of his system, notably Adele T. Katz (1946) and Felix Salzer (1952).[83] These works, however, are attempts to explain and clarify Schenker's entire system, and they properly belong more to a study of structural theory. Of more interest here is the influence that Schenker's work has had on the study of harmony and on works on purely harmonic theory in America.

The earliest American harmony text to avail itself of Schenker's theory is William Mitchell's *Elementary Harmony* (1939). Mitchell studied at Columbia University, where he received his M.A. in 1938. He joined the faculty at Columbia in 1932 and taught there until his retirement. *Elementary Harmony* represents an interesting mixture of elements of Schenker's early theory and his mature work.

Mitchell begins with an exposition of the harmonic series, from which he extracts the first six harmonics. Of the intervals formed by these harmonics, that of the perfect fifth has the greatest significance, because it represents the closest relationship between two different tones. Mitchell states that a series of such fifths is projected upward from the tonic, as in Figure 147; these tones are used as chord roots. In the harmonic series of C, the D is thus directly related to C as the ninth harmonic, whereas in Mitchell's system, D is indirectly related to C through G: "Harmonically, if we want to move from a chord built on D to one built on C we go via the intermediate G chord."[84]

Figure 147.   Mitchell, p. 3

Although Mitchell's procedure strongly resembles that of Goetschius's, there is no doubt that the origin of Mitchell's theory is Schenker's *Harmonielehre*. This is evident when Mitchell presents his theory of harmonic progression. He constructs a triad on each tone in a progression of ascending fifths upward to B, then continues up a diminished fifth to F, and thus back to C, as in Figure 148. He also shows the reverse progression from C downward. Mitchell notes, as did Schenker in *Harmonielehre*, that the unnatural diminished fifth between VII and IV acts as a dividing point in the series of fifths by directing the harmonic motion either up or down toward the tonic.[85]

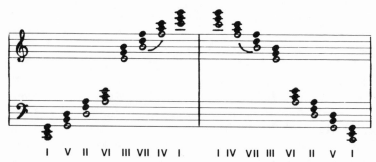

I V II VI III VII IV I   I IV VII III VI II V I

Figure 148.   Mitchell, p. 60

Mitchell observes that the progression in descending fifths "carries much more conviction" than that in which the fifths ascend. "The reason for this is that the progression of roots stands in the relation of an overtone to its ground tone. Hence, when the final tonic is reached the effect is that of an overtone (root of the V) reaching the final ground tone (root of the I). . . . In the ascending form (IV–I) just the opposite is the case: the final I is in effect like an overtone of the IV, hence less clear in its finality."[86] Thus Mitchell supplies a reasonable explanation for the natural downward tendency of the fifth-progression, an explanation which both Schenker and Goetschius might have used to good advantage. This explanation had not been advanced since Rameau stated in the *Traité de l'harmonie* that in a downward fifth-progression, the fifth "returns to its source."[87]

Mitchell regards root movement other than by fifths as ornamental. According to him, root movement of a third may be used to interpolate a chord into a fifth-progression, as the VI is interpolated between the I and the IV at *a* in Figure 149. Also, a root movement of a third may be used to transform a dissonance in the melody into a consonance. At *b*, for instance, the soprano note B forms a dissonance with the C major harmony against which it sounds; this dissonance is eliminated by interpolating the chord III between the I and the IV. Root movement of a second may be used to eliminate dissonance in a manner similar to that in which the third progression is used. Mitchell also mentions the possibility of regarding root progression by a second as a neighboring-tone relationship.

Figure 149. Mitchell, p. 66

The major triad is, of course, derived from the first six harmonics of the harmonic series. Mitchell's explanation of the minor triad is identical to Schenker's. Mitchell states that if a major triad were erected on each step of the major scale, as at *a* in Figure 150, the F-sharp, C-sharp, G-sharp, and D-sharp would conflict with the scale tones F, C, G, and D; the triads II, III, VI, and VII are altered to conform to the constituency of the scale, as at *b*. Since the triad on the seventh degree has two of its members thus altered, Mitchell states that it has suffered most by this process. Thus, VII is the weakest and least convincing of the triads.[88]

Figure 150.   Mitchell, p. 38

Evidence of Schenker's more mature theory is found in Mitchell's exposition of the scales. Mitchell considers the first, third, and fifth degrees of the major scale to be "principal tones," while the others are "dependent tones."[89] In this manner Mitchell relates the entire melodic content of the major key to the tonic triad, in a manner perfectly consistent with Schenker's concept that all music is a projection of a tonic triad. The "dependent tones" may move toward principal tones as passing tones, as in Figure 151*a*, or may ornament principal tones in the manner of neighboring tones, as at *b*.[90]

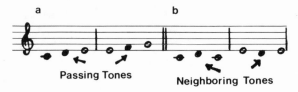

Figure 151.   Mitchell, p. 6

Mitchell considers the minor mode, like the major, to be a natural phenomenon. The natural minor mode is formed by a chain of fifths, as shown in Figure 152. However, he notes that the diminished fifth—here between VI and II—does not direct the harmonic motion toward I. It is therefore necessary to "correct" the minor scale by raising the seventh degree so that it forms a diminished fifth with the fourth degree, as in the major mode. This artificially formed diminished fifth now acts as it did in major, dividing harmonic motion into either upward or downward movement toward the tonic.[91]

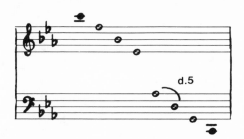

Figure 152. Mitchell, p. 100

Mitchell states that chords in the first inversion may be used as substitutes for their root-position triads or in conjunction with them. A first-inversion chord may also be used as a neighboring chord, as in progression I–V6–I. The second inversion chords are unstable chords, since they result from what Mitchell calls "secondary consonances." The perfect fourth is a secondary consonance, for instance, because it is not found naturally between the root and a harmonic in the harmonic series; it results from the inversion of such a natural interval. Thus, the perfect fourth in a second-inversion chord lends an element of instability to the chord, which thus depends on its context for its meaning. The second-inversion chord may appear as a formation of passing or neighboring tones, as in Figure 153a and b, or the bass itself may appear as a passing tone, as at c.[92]

According to Mitchell, the seventh-chord results from the addition of a melodic factor to a triad. The seventh appears as a passing or neighboring tone or a suspension, which, through usage, has come to be considered a part of the chord.[93] Similarly, the ninth-chord is actually formed by two appropriate nonharmonic tones over a triad.

The full impact of Schenker's theory surfaces in Mitchell's treatment of modulation. Mitchell points out that the

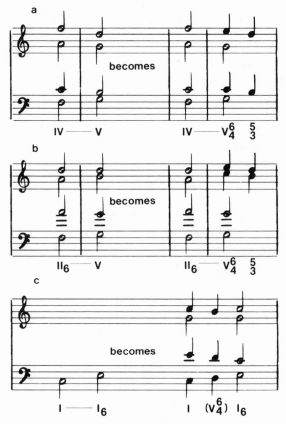

Figure 153. Mitchell, pp. 109, 112

relationship of various keys in a composition is the same type of relationship that individual chords bear to each other in a more localized context. "Modulation expands chordal relationships to the degree where a chord contributes not merely itself to musical expression, but all the characteristics of the key in which it is a tonic. For example, C major may be expressed by the chord progression tonic (I)-dominant (V)-tonic (I), or by the key progression, tonic key (C)-dominant key (G)-tonic key (C)."[94] Mitchell makes a careful distinction between the tonality, or tonic key, of a composition, and the other keys through which the composition may modulate.

Mitchell concludes his exposition of modulation with

examples of analysis in which he uses Schenker's graphic procedure. In Figure 154, for instance, Mitchell analyzes the scherzo from Beethoven's Sonata, Opus 28 (excluding the trio). At *a*, Mitchell shows the general modulatory scheme of the work, I–V–I, a genuine Schenkerian *Ursatz* progression. At *b* a more detailed illustration is given of the movement from I to V in the first section; *c* shows the middle section, in which the V becomes

Figure 154. Mitchell, pp. 222–23

V7 through movement of the inner voices; and *d* shows the detail of the final section, in which the tonic is reasserted.[95] The illustrations at *b*, *c*, and *d* are thus analogous to Schenker's *Mittelgrund*. By modern standards, such an analysis is not especially remarkable. It is quite surprising, however, to find Schenker's analytical procedure being used in a harmony textbook published as early as 1939.

An isolated feature of Schenker's theory, the concept of "tonicization," appears in Roger Sessions's *Harmonic Practice*. Sessions applies the term "tonicization" more liberally than Schenker. To Sessions, tonicization of a particular triad may involve anything from a single secondary dominant preceding the triad to a substantial section of a phrase in the key of which the triad is the tonic. However, Sessions is quite careful to make a distinction between tonicization and a genuine modulation. The process of tonicization, he states, establishes "secondary relationships within the orbit of the key,"[96] whereas a genuine modulation actually succeeds in establishing a new tonal center which does not sound dependent upon the original tonality.

According to Sessions, tonicization of a particular harmony may be achieved in one of two ways: through secondary dominants and secondary leading-tone chords, and also through altered accessory tones. A chord may be tonicized by a single secondary dominant or by a short series of secondary harmonies, as demonstrated in Figure 155. On a smaller scale, accessory tones may be altered to conform to the key of the chord which they embellish, achieving a very local degree of tonicization.

Concepts of Schenker's mature theory may be found in Allen Forte's *Tonal Harmony in Concept and Practice* (1962). Forte studied at Columbia University and received his M.A. there. He taught at Mannes School of Music and the Manhattan School of Music before his appointment to the faculty of Yale University. His works include *Contemporary Tone-Structures* (1955) and *The Compositional Matrix* (1961).

Forte begins *Tonal Harmony* with an exposition of the major scale. His treatment of the scale is remarkably similar to Mitchell's. Using as an example the theme from Beethoven's "Archduke" Trio shown in Figure 156, Forte notes that the accented degrees are the first, third, fifth, and eighth, spelling the

Figure 155.   Beethoven, "Hammerklavier" Sonata (Sessions, p. 255)

tonic triad.[97] In this manner, Forte illustrates the projection of the tonic harmony through all melodic activity. Unlike Mitchell, however, Forte carries his demonstration to the minor mode as well, using the theme from Bach's Harpsichord Concerto in D Minor, shown at *b*, to illustrate the influence of the tonic harmony in the minor scale.[98] The notes of the tonic triad are thus the stable tones of the scale, and they constitute the goals of melodic motion. After the tonic, the fifth scale degree is the most important; Forte notes that it divides the scale into two parts.

Figure 156.   Beethoven, "Archduke" Trio, Opus 97 (Forte, p. 3); Bach, Harpsichord Concerto in D minor (Forte, p. 7)

Forte defines a chord as a structure of at least three tones sounding simultaneously. He stipulates that a chord, to be recognized as such, must have at least the value of a full metrical pulse.[99] The basic chord formation is the triad. He constructs a diatonic triad on every degree of the major scale, including VII. In the minor mode he recognizes both the major and minor dominant and the major and diminished triads on the seventh degree. He states that "the leading tone is not included as a chord note in chords whose fundamental notes lie below scale degree 5."[100] Thus, he excludes the augmented form of the triad III, remarking that it is not a functional diatonic triad; the only form of the III in minor is the major triad. Forte also mentions that the major triad IV, drawn from the melodic minor scale, is used occasionally in minor.

The triad may generate other chord formations by three processes: the harmonic process, the melodic process, and the rhythmic process. The harmonic process of chord generation produces the inversion. Forte states that a chord in inversion may be used either as an extension of its parent triad, as in Figure 157*a*, or as a substitute for it, as in *b*. Forte states that not all first-inversion formations are considered harmonic equivalents of their parent triads; some of them result from linear motion, as will be seen. Second-inversion chords admit of a similar explanation.[101]

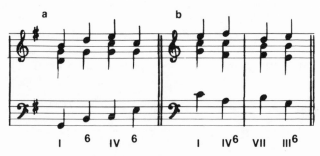

Figure 157.   Forte, pp. 69, 72

The melodic process of chord generation produces the seventh-chords. Forte's explanation of the evolution of the seventh-chord is similar to Piston's; the seventh first appeared as a passing dissonance, as in Figure 158*a*, and was eventually

assimilated into the harmony, as at *b*.[102] Forte recognizes four
types of seventh-chords: the major seventh, the minor seventh,
the dominant seventh, and the half-diminished seventh. He
considers the fully diminished seventh-chord to arise from the
melodic elaboration of the dominant seventh in first inversion, as
shown in Figure 159.[103] Of the ninth chords, he treats only that
on the dominant.

Figure 158.   Forte, p. 136

Figure 159.   Forte, p. 174

Rhythmic generation produces the "suspension
chord," a formation caused by the absorption of a suspension into
the harmony. The example in Figure 160*a* shows a suspension C,

Figure 160.   Gluck, Orfeo (Forte, pp. 310–11)

at the asterisk. If the duration of the suspension is lengthened to at least the value of a full metric pulse, as at *b*, the entire combination—suspension and all—is regarded as a harmony.[104]

To the chords generated by the three processes already mentioned, Forte adds a fourth category, "linear chords," which he says are those that "are described most easily in terms of the linear, or melodic, functions of their notes."[105] The simplest type of diatonic linear chord is that formed by passing tones, as at the asterisk in Figure 161. Forte states that in such a chord, "We need not concern ourselves with describing the vertical intervals. We need only know that the chord is produced by passing notes."[106]

Figure 161. Forte, p. 341

Not all linear chords are dissonant. Certain first-inversion chords, such as the one in Figure 162, are comprehended as linear combinations, rather than as substitutes for their parent chords. Second-inversion chords are also described as linear formations. Chromatic linear chords include the augmented dominant and the chords of the augmented sixths.

Figure 162. Schubert, Du Bist die Ruhe (Forte, p. 350)

Schenker's theory comes to the fore in Forte's explanation of harmonic progression. Forte notes that the fifth is the only interval which absolutely defines the triad (his demonstration is shown in Figure 163), and that the fifth between the tonic and the dominant similarly defines the tonality.[107] "The triads I and V are called primary triads, to indicate their primary function described above. Those on the remaining scale degrees are called secondary triads."[108] Thus, Forte breaks with the Rameau tradition by relegating the subdominant to the class of secondary triads. The two primary triads become the basis of Forte's theory of harmonic progression.

Figure 163.   Forte, p. 87

Forte discusses root movement by fifths, by seconds, and by thirds. Root movement by fifths is, of course, the strongest, by analogy with the fifth between I and V. Included in this class of root movement is that by the interval of a diminished fifth, as IV–VII. Root movement by seconds is next in order of importance: "We will characterize this stepwise interval of bass progression as melodic."[109] Thus, in the progression IV–V, the root of the secondary chord IV relates as an auxiliary or passing tone to the root of the V. The last in the hierarchy of root movement is that by thirds.

In the example in Figure 164, then, the most important relationships are those between the principal triads, that is, the fifth (or fourth) relationship between I and V and between V and I, as at *a*. At *b*, a IV is inserted to precede V; the IV forms a second or neighboring relationship with V. The VI added at *c* forms third relationships with the I and the IV; of greater importance than these third relationships, however, is the second relationship it forms as an upper neighbor to V.[110]

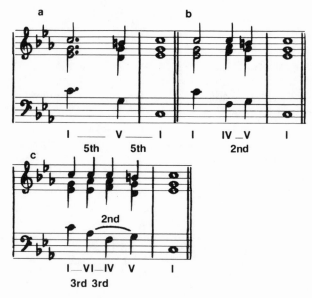

Figure 164. Forte, p. 91

Forte states: "Essentially there are two harmonic directions: toward I and toward V. These primary diatonic triads form the harmonic axis of tonal music."[111] He presents a sample model of this harmonic axis to show how other chords in a progression may relate to the harmonic goals I and V.

Figure 165. Model of harmonic axis (Forte, p. 99)

Forte's harmonic axis is, of course, nothing less than a Schenkerian *Ursatz* progression. Forte further states that, besides I and V, other chords are possible harmonic goals under certain conditions. A dominant preparation, such as II or IV, may act as an intermediate goal, from which the harmony proceeds on to V. A secondary triad may also become a "quasi-tonic" by means of modulation. "Under this condition it then has its own secondary triads and controls a harmonic domain in the same way as the main triad."[112] The best example of this is the triad III in minor, which is reached by a modulation to the relative major key.[113]

In order to reach a harmonic goal, the harmony must follow one of three types of progressions: circular progression, opening progression, or closing progression. Although Forte does not specify the dimension of these progressions, he seems to imply that a single progression occupies the length of a phrase, with the harmonic goal represented at the cadence. A circular progression "departs from a chord and has as its goal the same chord—for example, I–I or V–V."[114] An opening progression departs from a chord—usually I—and has as its goal a different chord, such as I–II or I–V. A closing progression is one that returns to I. The three types of progressions are illustrated in Figure 166.

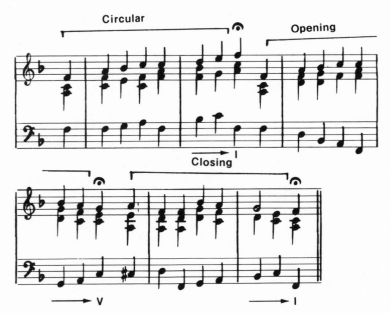

Figure 166. Chorale "O Ewigkeit, du Donner wort" (Forte, p. 105)

It is too early to assess the full impact of Schenker's theory on the study of harmony in the United States. Since the publication of Forte's *Tonal Harmony* in 1962, more recent harmony texts have incorporated some of Schenker's ideas. This trend may be expected to continue as Schenker's works become increasingly accessible to American musicians. It is unlikely that Schenker's theory will ever entirely replace the procedures that have become established in the study of harmony in the United States, because its aims simply are not the same. Nonetheless, there is no doubt that Schenker's ideas, as in the past, will continue to contribute to American musicians' concept of harmony.

5
Conclusion

The traditions that have been establishing themselves since 1941 appear to be continuing. The philosophy of Walter Piston, for instance, is reflected in Paul Harder's popular *Harmonic Materials in Tonal Music* (1968); in fact, Harder defines the historical period under observation as 1600–1900, his equivalent of Piston's period of "common practice."[1] While Robert Ottman's *Elementary Harmony* and *Advanced Harmony* (1961) do not present McHose's detailed statistical approach, Ottman does at least remain faithful to many of McHose's conclusions. Elements of Schenker's theory are appearing more frequently in theory texts since the appearance of Allen Forte's work in 1962. While many experiments may be seen in the pedagogical aspects of harmony texts, the harmonic theory they convey seems to be developing along easily recognizable lines of tradition.

Amid all the developments in the post-1941 traditions there is no real revival of acoustical theory as the basis for a system of harmony, nor does any such trend appear to be on the horizon. The major triad and major scale are now seen as phenomena traditional within a period of "common practice" rather than as "nature's harmony" or "nature's scale." One of the reasons for the rejection of acoustics may well be that its possible contributions to the study of harmony appear to be exhausted. The harmonic series provides the theorist with an excellent explanation of the tonic and dominant functions and the major triad; it provides no justification at all for the subdominant function or the minor triad.

Another reason for the decline in interest in acoustical theory appears to be the result of the development of the harmonic usage in music since 1900. Acoustical explanations may be feasible for such twentieth-century phenomena as quartal harmony or polychordal combinations, but what of tone-clusters, or of harmony using microtonal intervals? A great deal of explanation would be required to present these as "chords of nature," and if they can be used successfully without an obvious foundation in the harmonic series, might it be unnecessary to worry about the natural origin of the triad and the seventh-chord? Also, as musical scholarship progresses, musicians are becoming less convinced of the supremacy of the tonal system of the last two centuries. If the major triad is indeed a "natural" harmony, why was it not used by the ancient Greeks or the ninth-century ecclesiastical musicians? Why is it not found in the traditional music of China, Africa, or the Middle East?

The last objection appears to be the weakest. Acoustical theory was, of course, well known to the ancient Greeks and the medieval theorists, who used it for melodic, rather than harmonic, purposes. When harmony began to develop, acoustical theory played an important part by defining only the simplest intervals as permissible consonances. Moreover, as Donald Tweedy observed, the musical systems of most cultures have an acoustically perfect fifth in some important position in their tonal framework. The ancient Greeks and ancient Chinese arrived at their perfect fifth through the mathematical division of a vibrating body. But what of the perfect fifths found in some African scales? What of the perfect fifth which occurs in the various Indian *ragas*? These are not calculated through mathematical acoustics, yet they have arisen as important intervals anyway. The spontaneity of the perfect fifth in these systems may be a rather telling argument in favor of a revival of acoustics as a legitimate basis of theory.

The most important development in the study of diatonic harmony by American theorists is the concept of harmonic progression. The most normal progression is that in which the chord root moves in descending perfect fifths until the tonic is reached; any other harmonic movement is unusual or irregular. This seems to be the consensus of American theorists, whether they establish it by acoustical means (Goetschius and

Robinson), by analogy with the authentic cadence (Piston and Goldman), or simply by observation of its relative frequency of occurrence (McHose). There is no lack of support for it no matter how it is established. The descending-fifth pattern occurs frequently enough in musical practice of the eighteenth and nineteenth centuries that it can certainly be considered normal by the standard of observation. The analogy with the authentic cadence seems logical enough. The acoustical basis of the pattern is also sound; by admitting one essential condition, the establishment of the tonic as the most important tone, the roots of other chords are perceived as harmonic partials, which demand roots a fifth below, which in turn are heard as partials demanding their roots, until the tonic is reached.

American theorists have had less success in explaining the inclusion of the subdominant in the pattern of descending fifths. It has been seen that Goetschius began by placing the subdominant a fifth below the tonic, but his theory finally forced him to reposition it in his Second Class, as a chord derived from the supertonic, or "second dominant." Robinson and Tweedy seem to have followed him to a certain extent. But by accounting for the subdominant as a part of the supertonic, a theorist is left without a good explanation of the plagal cadence. This cadence then becomes II_7°—I, a most unlikely departure from the normal progression of descending fifths. On the other hand, a theorist who considers the subdominant to be a legitimate position a fifth below the tonic is left without a realistic acoustical explanation of its origin. The lack of acoustical reality does not seem to affect theorists such as Piston and McHose, who limit their procedures to observation of practice. Yet even they cannot avoid classifying the subdominant with the supertonic in order to explain the frequent occurrence of the progression IV–V.

The most logical solution to the "subdominant problem" seems to be the idea that there are, in fact, two IV chords: one is derived from II7 and normally precedes V; the other is somehow a fifth below the tonic and acts as an ornamentation of the I. Ortmann, in advancing his explanation, states that the plagal subdominant has no real harmonic function and is only ornamental. Goldman offers a similar explanation, saying that the subdominant is "not in reality relevant to traditional design."[2] But the plagal cadence *does* project the effect of a fifth-relationship with the tonic, although the IV here lacks the strong downward impulse of the other fifths in the scheme of normal progression. Perhaps the best explanation of the plagal subdominant is that it does indeed lie a fifth beneath the tonic; this fifth, however, is not established acoustically from the tonic, but by analogy with the other fifths in the pattern of normal progression.

Theorists who have simply observed practice seem to have had considerably less difficulty with the minor mode than those who have attempted to justify it acoustically. A writer who is observing musical practice may cite the history of the scales and the development of the minor mode from the old ecclesiastical modes, or he may construct the minor scale from three principal triads, all or some of which are minor. Theorists, like Goetschius and Robinson, who worked from an acoustical basis are forced to conclude that the minor mode is somehow less natural than the major.

The domain of chromatically altered harmony has been shrinking in American theory since the nineteenth century. Richter's *Lehrbuch* had allowed any chromatic alterations, but Goetschius limited such alteration to only certain scale degrees, so that the changes would not interfere with the normal progression of chords by fifths. Robinson and Tweedy followed Goetschius in this respect. Piston further reduced the concept of alteration by introducing the secondary dominant as a genuine function and by considering the parallel mode a legitimate part of the tonality. Since Piston, theorists have increasingly been inclined to regard any nondiatonic combination as a linear development of the original diatonic chord, rather than an actual alteration of one of the chord tones.

The classification of nonharmonic tones has been handled in various ways. Some theorists, such as Wedge and McHose, retained the old European system of classifying nonharmonic tones solely according to the manner in which the tones enter and progress. Other American writers, such as Robinson, Tweedy, and Piston, have recognized the significance of the rhythmic placement of certain nonharmonic types, especially the appoggiatura, and have accordingly tried to group the nonharmonic types into larger categories of "accented" and "unaccented" tones. Although a standard system of rhythmic classification of nonharmonic tones is not yet recognized among American theorists, the awareness of the influence of rhythmic accent has added an important consideration to the study of these tones.

Finally there remains the matter of analytical symbols.[3] There are basically two traditions in the development of these symbols. The first tradition dates from the appearance of the works of Weber and Richter in America and uses Weber's system of uppercase and lowercase Roman numerals. To this system has been added the practice of showing inversions by means of figured-bass numerals. Chromatic alterations are shown by accidentals next to appropriate figured-bass numerals, so that an altered tone is considered in its relation to the chord. Alongside this system has developed another, stemming from the Goetschius tradition. In it, only uppercase Roman numerals are used and inversions are shown by Goetschius's system of subscript arabic numerals. Chromatic alterations are not shown as altered chord members, but are understood as altered scale degrees.

Of the two systems, the one stemming from the Goetschius tradition seems to be declining in popularity, while the Weber-Richter system, with refinements, has become universally recognized. The most conspicuous contribution of the Goetschius system seems to be the use of only uppercase Roman numerals, which sometimes may be seen with figured-bass symbols. Other aspects of the Goetschius system are regarded as obsolete. Even McHose's use of arabic numerals to specify altered scale degrees has become infrequent. Wallace Berry uses McHose's system in *Form in Music* in 1966; however, more significant than its appearance is the fact that Berry finds it necessary to explain the symbolization in a footnote.[4]

However diverse the various contributions of American theorists may be, there can be no question that they have added much of value to the study of harmony. Richard Franko Goldman may jokingly state, "When all is considered, one is tempted to say that, for most of the objectives of traditional harmony study, the old standard text of Ernst Richter . . . is probably as good as any."[5] But Goldman realizes, as do most American writers, that many new concepts have been proposed and have found their way into the common body of knowledge of harmonic theory since Richter's time. Without the contributions of American theorists there might be no accepted theory of harmonic progression, no recognition of the functions of many types of chromatic harmony, and no appreciation of the influence of rhythm on harmony, to cite only a few features. Of course, Richter's text is no longer "as good as any" as an exposition of harmonic theory. American theorists have had too many good ideas since.

Notes

Chapter 1

1. James F. Warner, "Translator's Preface," in Gottfried Weber, *Theory of Musical Composition*, p. xi.
2. Warner, "Translator's Preface," in Weber, p. xiii.
3. *Dwight's Journal of Music* 1 (May 1, 1852): 29.
4. *Dwight's Journal of Music* 34 (July 25, 1874): 270.
5. *Dwight's Journal of Music* 7 (December 22, 1855): 94.
6. Stainer's exposition of his harmonic theory is given in his *Theory of Harmony Founded on the Tempered Scale* (London: Novello & Co., 1871).
7. Weber, p. 222.
8. Ibid., p. 224.
9. Matthew Shirlaw, *The Theory and Nature of Harmony*, p. 9.
10. Hugo Riemann, *History of Music Theory*, Vol. 3, trans. William Mickelson, p. 198.
11. Weber, p. 169.
12. Ibid.
13. Ibid., p. 20.
14. "But men have not only created for themselves an art of speech and of tones; they have also scientifically investigated the nature of sound, and have referred to its physical and mathematical principles (Acoustics, the Doctrine of Sound)." Weber, p. 20.
15. Ibid., p. 22.
16. Ibid., p. 16.
17. Ibid., p. 23.
18. Ibid.
19. Rameau, *Nouveau Système*, Chapter 6, quoted in Shirlaw, p. 143.
20. Weber, p. 24.
21. Ibid., p. 123.
22. Ibid., p. 169.
23. Ibid., p. 230.
24. Ibid., p. 210.

25. Ibid., p. 208.
26. Ibid., p. 209.
27. Ibid., p. 260.
28. Ibid., p. 261.
29. Ibid.
30. Ibid., p. 234.
31. Ibid., p. 309.
32. Ibid., p. 311.
33. Ibid., p. 316.
34. Ibid., p. 317.
35. Ibid., p. 329.
36. Ibid., p. 330.
37. Ibid., p. 171.
38. Abt Vogler was actually the first to use Roman numerals to indicate chord roots. Weber's important contribution was the development of these symbols to indicate the chord quality as well as the root. G. T. Jones, *Symbols Used in Music Analysis*, p. 309.
39. Shirlaw, p. 333.
40. Riemann (Mickelson), p. 210.
41. Warner, in Weber, p. xii.
42. Riemann, *Musik Lexikon*, Vol. II, p. 500 (s.v. "Richter, E. F.").
43. Ernst F. Richter, *Manual of Harmony*, trans. John P. Morgan, p. vi.
44. Ibid., p. 22.
45. Ibid., p. 40.
46. Ibid., p. 42.
47. Ibid., p. 43.
48. Ibid., p. 64.
49. Ibid., p. 123.
50. Ibid., p. 128.
51. Ibid.
52. Ibid., p. 138.
53. Ibid., p. 140.
54. Riemann, *Musik Lexikon*, s.v. "Faisst, Immanuel Gottlob," p. 486.
55. Immanuel Faisst, Preface in Percy Goetschius, *The Material Used in Musical Composition*, p. ix.
56. Immanuel Faisst, *Harmonielehre nach Immanuel Faisst*, adapted by Heinrich Lang.
57. "Am wichtigsten für den Ausdruck einer Tonart sind die Dreiklänge I (tonischer Dreiklang), V (Dominantdreiklang), und IV (Subdominant-dreiklang) (I als Zentrum, V als höheres, IV als tieferes Gebeit der Tonart). Sie werden Hauptdreiklänge genannt. In diesen Hauptdreiklänge ist die ganze Tonart gegeben." Faisst, *Harmonielehre*, p. 13.
58. "Der Übergang vom I auf den V macht auf das harmonische Gefühle die Wirkung einer Hebung und Anregung. Die umgekehrte Verbindung V I gibt die Wirkung einer Senkung und Beruhigung des harmonischen Gefühls und ist deshalb geeignet, regelmässig zum Abschluss eines Stückes verwendet zu werden." Ibid., p. 16.
59. "Da sich I zu IV verhält wie V zu I, so macht die Folge I IV (mit

kadenzierender Bassfolge) die Wirkung der Senkung und Beruhigung, sie wird daher häufig dem Ganzschluss angehängt, natürlich mit Rückkehr in den I." Ibid., p. 18.

60. "Die Nebendreiklänge heissen so, weil sie für den Ausdruck der Tonart weniger geeignet erscheinen. Am meisten tonale Kraft haben sie noch da, wo sie als Vertreter von Hauptdreiklängen wirken. Von den konsonierenden Nebendreiklängen steht nun jeder in naher Bezeihung zu dem Hauptdreiklang, der eine kleine Terz höher steht:

der VI in Dur und Moll zum I,
der II in Dur zum IV,
der III in Dur zum V

derart, dass der Nebendreiklänge gerne als Stellvertreter oder nachfolgender Begleiter des Hauptdreiklanges dient." Ibid., p. 19.

61. Ibid., p. 22.

62. Ibid., p. 61.

63. "Jeder dissonierende Akkord findet seine regelmässige Auflösung in einem Akkord, dessen Grundton eine Quinte tiefer oder eine Quarte höher steht als der dissonierenden, so dass die Folge der Grundtöne die natürlichste Grundbassfolge darstellt, nämlich die kadenzierende." Ibid., p. 37.

64. Ibid., p. 66.

65. Ibid., p. 45.

66. Ibid., p. 24.

67. Alfred Day, *A Treatise on Harmony*, p. 51.

68. Ibid.

69. Ibid.

70. Frederick Ouseley, *A Treatise on Harmony*, p. 15.

71. Ibid., p. 20.

72. Shirlaw, p. 430.

73. Ouseley, p. 123.

74. Ibid.

75. Ibid.

76. Ibid., p. 68.

77. Ebenezer Prout, *Harmony, its Theory and Practice*, pp. 35–36.

78. Shirlaw, p. 444.

79. George A. Macfarren, *Six Lectures on Harmony*, 3rd ed., p. 221.

80. Prout, p. 38.

81. Ibid.

82. Ouseley, p. 142.

83. Prout, p. 215.

84. Ouseley, pp. 41–43.

85. Prout, p. 157.

86. Ibid., p. 155.

87. Ibid., p. 172.

88. Ibid., p. 121.

89. Ibid., p. 154.

90. Ibid., p. 155.

91. Prout, p. 192. The same explanation of this chord is given by Macfarren in *Six Lectures*, p. 175.

92. Day, p. 121; Ouseley, p. 126; Prout, p. 199.
93. Ouseley, p. 163.
94. Prout, p. 111.
95. Ibid., p. 221.
96. Ibid., p. 225.
97. Richter, p. 118.
98. Ouseley, p. 197; Prout, p. 261.
99. Prout, p. 115.
100. Ouseley, p. 204.
101. Ibid., p. 58.
102. Ibid., p. 117.
103. Prout, p. 103.
104. Ibid., p. 101.
105. Ibid., p. 102.
106. Ibid., pp. 75–76.
107. Ibid., p. 108.
108. Shirlaw, p. 444.
109. Prout, *Harmony, its Theory and Practice*, 16th ed. (London: Augener & Co., 1901), Preface, p. vii.

Chapter 2

1. G. T. Jones, *Symbols Used in Music Analysis*, p. 916.
2. For a detailed account of Goetschius's life and a critical examination of his work, see "Percy Goetschius: An American Theorist and Teacher" by Mother Catherine Agnes Carroll (Ph.D. diss., University of Rochester, 1957), to which the present biographical sketch is indebted. A personal view of Goetschius during his career is found in Arthur Shepherd, " 'Papa' Goetschius in Retrospect," *Musical Quarterly* 30 (1944), 307–18.
3. Shepherd, p. 314.
4. Carroll, p. 29.
5. Ibid., p. 24.
6. Mason, in Shepherd, pp. 34–35.
7. Carroll, pp. 34–35.
8. Goetschius, *The Material Used in Musical Composition*, p. 11. This and subsequent references refer to the 11th edition, issued in 1910.
9. Ibid.
10. Ibid.
11. Ibid., p. 12.
12. Ibid., Preface, p. vi.
13. Equal temperament was standard in Germany by 1800, in France and the United States by 1850.
14. The cent system, introduced by Sir Alexander Ellis (1814–1890), is an

arbitrary division of the octave into 1,200 equal intervals, called cents. Thus a tempered semitone measures 100 cents.

15. Goetschius, *Material Used*, pp. 12–13.
16. Percy Goetschius, *The Theory and Practice of Tone-Relations*, p. 5.
17. Ibid., p. 6.
18. Ibid., p. 15.
19. Ibid., p. 15.
20. The acoustical nonexistence of the subdominant is discussed in Prout, *Harmony, its Theory and Practice*, p. 36.
21. Goetschius, *Material Used*, p. 3.
22. Ibid., p. 6. The terminology of this concept appears to be borrowed from F. J. Fétis, who, however, used it quite differently. Fétis's "notes of repose" are the first, fourth, and fifth, and sometimes the sixth scale degrees, based on their capacity to support a perfect fifth. Shirlaw, *Theory and Nature of Harmony*, pp. 340–45.
23. Goetschius, *Material Used*, p. 6.
24. Goetschius, *Material Used*, p. 22.
25. Goetschius, *Tone-Relations*, p. 14.
26. Goetschius, *Material Used*, p. 23.
27. Ibid., Preface, p. vi.
28. Ibid., p. 39.
29. Ibid., p. 40.
30. Ibid.
31. Ibid., p. 45.
32. Goetschius's Example 24 is shown in Figure 35.
33. Goetschius, *Material Used*, p. 27.
34. Ibid., p. 32.
35. Ibid.
36. Ibid., p. 37.
37. Ibid., p. 38.
38. Ibid., p. 50.
39. Ibid., p. 72.
40. Goetschius, *Tone-Relations*, p. 62.
41. Goetschius, *Material Used*, p. 72.
42. Ibid., p. 14.
43. Ibid., p. 98.
44. Ibid., p. 92.
45. Goetschius, *Tone-Relations*, p. 85.
46. Ibid., p. 86.
47. Ibid., p. 85.
48. Goetschius, *Material Used*, p. 109.
49. Jean-Philippe Rameau, *Traité de l'harmonie*, Book 2, p. 50.
50. Arthur Loesser, in Shepherd, p. 313.
51. Goetschius, *Material Used*, p. 124.
52. Ibid., pp. 125–26.
53. Ibid., p. 126.
54. Ibid., pp. 128–30. Although the system presented in *Material Used* and *Tone-*

Relations does not admit the use of the Neapolitan sixth-chord in major,
Goetschius does admit this possibility in "The Lowered Second Scale Step,"
Etude 3 (1935), p. 574.

55. Goetschius, *Material Used*, p. 132.
56. Ibid., p. 133.
57. Ibid., p. 124.
58. Ibid., p. 123.
59. Ibid., Preface, p. x.
60. Goetschius, *Tone-Relations*, p. 101.
61. Goetschius, *Material Used*, p. 124. Cf. Prout, p. 103.
62. Ibid., p. 137.
63. Goetschius, *Tone-Relations*, p. 97.
64. Ibid., p. 99.
65. Goetschius, *Material Used*, p. 180.
66. Ibid.
67. See p. 49.
68. Goetschius, *Material Used*, p. 139.
69. Ibid.
70. Ibid.
71. Ibid., p. 140.
72. Ibid.
73. Ibid.
74. Ibid., p. 143.
75. Ibid., p. 158.
76. Ibid.
77. Ibid., p. 160.
78. Carroll, p. 67.
79. Goetschius, *Material Used*, p. 270.
80. Goetschius, *Tone-Relations*, p. 135.
81. Ibid., p. 12.
82. Goetschius, *Material Used*, p. 185.
83. Ibid.
84. Ibid.
85. Ibid.
86. Ibid.
87. Ibid., p. 190.
88. Ibid., p. 192. Goetschius uses as an example of an irregular organ point measures 34–47 of the second movement of Schumann's Third Symphony.
89. Ibid., p. 195.
90. Ibid., p. 197.
91. Ibid., p. 204.
92. Ibid., p. 209.
93. Ibid., p. 215. Cf. Prout, p. 119.
94. Goetschius, *Material Used*, p. 212.
95. Ibid., p. 217.
96. Ibid., p. 218.
97. Ibid., p. 219.
98. Ibid., p. 224.
99. Ibid., p. 225.

Chapter 3

1. Arthur E. Heacox, *Harmony for Ear, Eye, and Keyboard*, pp. 177–78.
2. Solomon Jadassohn, *Manual of Harmony*, trans. Paul Torek and H. B. Pasmore.
3. Frank Shepard, *Harmony Simplified*, p. 46.
4. George Chadwick, *Harmony*, p. 5.
5. Francis York, *Harmony Simplified*, p. 19.
6. Benjamin Cutter, *Harmonic Analysis*, p. 4.
7. Ebenezer Prout, *Harmony, its Theory and Practice*, 16th ed., p. 63.
8. Shepard, pp. 46–47.
9. Chadwick, p. 1.
10. Jadassohn, p. 13.
11. Shepard, p. 47; Chadwick, p. 118; Thomas Tapper, *First Year Harmony*, p. 43; Howard E. Parkhurst, *Harmony* p. 17.
12. Shepard, p. 105; Parkhurst, p. 59.
13. Cutter, p. 39.
14. Chadwick, p. 130.
15. Arthur Foote and Walter Spalding, *Modern Harmony in its Theory and Practice*, p. 117.
16. York, p. 60.
17. Carolyn Alchin, *Applied Harmony*, rev. Vincent Jones, 1: 64.
18. Foote and Spalding, p. 218.
19. Shepard, p. 205.
20. Shepard, pp. 43–44.
21. Chadwick, p. 74.
22. Chadwick, p. 190; cf. Prout (1889 ed.), p. 115.
23. York, p. 53.
24. Walter Spalding, *Tonal Counterpoint* (Boston: Arthur P. Schmidt, 1904), pp. 23, 204.
25. Foote and Spalding, pp. 6–7; cf. Prout (16th ed.), pp. 5–6. Spalding seems to have assumed Prout's literary style to a great extent; a number of Prout's stock phrases are echoed in *Modern Harmony*. The most conspicuous is a phrase Prout uses to introduce a musical illustration: "The following example will repay careful study," which appears in *Modern Harmony* as "The following examples will repay study" (p. 122), or "The following works will repay thorough analysis" (p. 252).
26. Ibid., pp. 166–69.
27. Ibid., p. 16.
28. See p. 29.
29. Foote and Spalding, p. 26.
30. Ibid., p. 36.
31. Ibid., p. 78.
32. Ibid., p. 202.
33. Ibid., p. 200.
34. Shepard, p. 91.
35. York, Introduction, p. iv.
36. Ibid., p. 2.
37. Ibid., pp. 34, 38.

38. Ibid., p. 38.
39. Ibid., p. 9.
40. Ibid., p. 45.
41. Ibid., p. 81.
42. Ibid., p. 86.
43. Ibid., p. 90.
44. Ibid., p. 2.
45. Ibid.
46. Ibid., p. 8.
47. Cutter, p. 3.
48. Ibid., p. 17.
49. Ibid., p. 1.
50. Ibid., p. 2.
51. Ibid., p. 4.
52. Ibid., p. 18.
53. Ibid.
54. Ibid., p. 31.
55. Ibid., p. 33.
56. Ibid., p. 35.
57. Ibid., p. 26.
58. Ibid., p. 29.
59. Ibid., p. 27.
60. Ibid., p. 25.
61. Louis Elson, *The History of American Music*, p. 357.
62. Franklin Robinson, *Aural Harmony*, rev. ed., 2 vols., Preface, p. xv.
63. Ibid., 1: 5.
64. Ibid.
65. Ibid., p. 11.
66. Ibid., p. 12.
67. Ibid.
68. Ibid.
69. Ibid., p. 94.
70. Ibid., p. 20.
71. Ibid.
72. Ibid., p. 32.
73. Ibid., p. 34.
74. Ibid., p. 65.
75. Ibid., p. 193.
76. Ibid., p. 74.
77. Ibid., p. 38.
78. Ibid., p. 41.
79. Ibid.
80. Ibid., pp. 47–48.
81. Ibid., p. 45.
82. Ibid., p. 137.
83. Ibid., 2: 4.
84. Ibid., 1: 235–37.
85. Ibid., p. 237.
86. Ibid., p. 240.

87. Ibid., 2: 66–67.
88. Ibid., 1: 127.
89. Otto Ortmann, "Notes on the Nature of Harmony" *Musical Quarterly,* 6 (July, 1921): 369.
90. Ibid., p. 371.
91. Ibid., p. 370.
92. Ibid., p. 375.
93. Publisher's Introduction, Donald Tweedy, *Manual of Harmonic Technique,* p. vii.
94. Tweedy, Preface, p. x.
95. Ibid., p. xii.
96. Although some ethnomusicological studies had been done by Americans prior to 1928, notably the work of Fewkes and Gilman, and Frances Densmore, the field was largely unsystematized until the introduction of Erich von Hornbostel's methods in the United States by his student G. Herzog, in 1928.
97. Tweedy, p. 1.
98. Ibid., p. 4.
99. Ibid., p. 5.
100. Ibid.
101. Ibid. p. 7.
102. Ibid., pp. 19–20.
103. Ibid., p. 22.
104. Ibid., pp. 22–23.
105. Ibid., pp. 88, 102.
106. Ibid., p. 164.
107. Ibid., p. 230.
108. Ibid., p. 236.
109. Ibid., p. 32.
110. Ibid., p. 154.
111. George Wedge, *Advanced Ear Training and Sight-Singing,* pp. 1–2, 43, 132, 229, and others.
112. Ibid., p. 2.
113. George Wedge, *Applied Harmony,* 1: 1.
114. Ibid., pp. 1–2.
115. Ibid., p. 2.
116. Ibid., p. 79.
117. Ibid., pp. 39–40.
118. Ibid., p. 42.
119. Ibid., p. 42.
120. Ibid., p. 109.
121. Wedge, *Applied Harmony,* 2: 36.
122. Ibid., p. 63.
123. Ibid., p. 79.
124. Ibid., p. 72.
125. Ibid., p. 91.
126. George Leighton, *Harmony, Analytical and Applied,* pp. 19, 93, 30.
127. Carl Paige Wood, *The Texture of Music,* pp. 37, 102, 30.
128. Carleton Bullis, *Harmonic Forms,* p. 40.

129. Percy Goetschius, *The Structure of Music*, p. 44.
130. York, p. 86.
131. Ibid., p. 87.
132. Ibid., p. 88.
133. Shepard, p. 165.
134. Ibid., p. 166.
135. Ibid., p. 182.
136. Cutter, pp. 15–17.
137. Ibid., p. 17.
138. Ibid., p. 42.
139. Cutter, Appendix, p. 113.
140. Ibid., p. 115.
141. Arthur Foote, *Modulation and Related Harmonic Questions*, p. 7.
142. Ibid., p. 8.
143. Tweedy, p. 27.
144. Ibid., p. 31.
145. Ibid., pp. 30–31.
146. Wedge, 1: 153.
147. Wedge, 2: iv.
148. Ibid., pp. 1, 22.
149. Ibid., p. 56.
150. Ibid., p. 22.
151. Bullis, p. 178.
152. William J. Mitchell, *Elementary Harmony*, p. 190.
153. Ibid., p. 191.
154. Walter Piston, *Principles of Harmonic Analysis*, p. 1.
155. Walter Piston, *Harmony*, p. 166.

Chapter 4

1. Walter Piston, *Harmony*, Introd., pp. ix–x.
2. Ibid., p. ix.
3. Ibid., p. 4.
4. Ibid., p. 32.
5. Ibid., p. 35.
6. Ibid., p. 17.
7. Ibid., p. 18.
8. Ibid.
9. Ibid., p. 19.
10. Ibid., p. 50.
11. Ibid., p. 54.
12. Ibid., p. 55.
13. Ibid., p. 96.
14. Ibid., pp. 96–105.
15. Ibid., p. 145.
16. Ibid., p. 140.

17. Ibid., p. 147.
18. Ibid., p. 152.
19. Ibid., p. 153.
20. Ibid., p. 160.
21. Ibid., p. 161.
22. Ibid., p. 259.
23. Ibid., p. 166. Emphasis mine.
24. Ibid., p. 288.
25. Ibid., p. 300.
26. Ibid., p. 301.
27. Ibid., pp. 303–5.
28. Ibid., p. 123.
29. Ibid., p. 130.
30. Ibid.
31. Ibid., pp. 132–33.
32. Ibid., p. 85.
33. Ibid., p. 86.
34. Ibid., p. 87.
35. Paul Hindemith, *Traditional Harmony*, 2 vols., 1: 82.
36. Roger Sessions, *Harmonic Practice*, p. 244.
37. Ibid., p. 245. The concept of nondominant secondary functions also appears in the third edition (1962) of Piston's *Harmony*, p. 328.
38. William Christ, et al., *Materials and Structure of Music*, 2 vols., 2: 95.
39. Wallace Berry, *Form in Music*, p. 249n.
40. Walter Piston, *Harmony*, 3rd ed. (New York: W. W. Norton, 1962), p. 331.
41. Sessions, p. 268.
42. Allen I. McHose, *The Contrapuntal Harmonic Technique of the 18th Century*, p. 144.
43. Sessions, p. 173.
44. Ibid., p. 225.
45. Ibid., p. 285.
46. Justine Shir-Clif, Stephen Jay, and Donald J. Rauscher, *Chromatic Harmony*, p. 46.
47. Sessions, p. 80.
48. Ibid., pp. 86–90.
49. Christ, et al., 1: 306.
50. Ibid.
51. Sessions, p. 6.
52. Ibid., Foreword, p. xiii.
53. Richard Franko Goldman, *Harmony in Western Music*, p. 30.
54. Ibid., p. 31.
55. Allen Irvine McHose, *Contrapuntal Harmonic Technique*, Preface, p. ix.
56. Ibid.
57. Ibid., p. 3.
58. Ibid., p. 4.
59. Ibid., p. 5.
60. Ibid.
61. Ibid., p. 9.
62. Ibid., p. 10.

63. Ibid., p. 11.
64. Ibid., p. 16.
65. Ibid., p. 17.
66. Ibid., p. 231.
67. Ibid., p. 234.
68. Ibid., pp. 118, 127.
69. Allen Irvine McHose, *Basic Principles of the Technique of 18th and 19th Century Composition*, pp. 105–7.
70. Ibid., p. 107.
71. Ibid., p. 105.
72. Ibid., p. 107.
73. Ibid., p. 199.
74. Heinrich Schenker, *Harmony*, trans. Elizabeth Mann Borgese.
75. Ibid., pp. 26–40.
76. Ibid., p. 49.
77. Ibid., p. 144.
78. Ibid., p. 188.
79. Ibid., p. 197.
80. Ibid., p. 157.
81. See Heinrich Schenker, *Der Freie Satz*, "Anhang," pp. 1–9.
82. Ibid., p. 50.
83. Adele T. Katz, *Challenge to Musical Tradition* (New York: Alfred A. Knopf, 1946); Felix Salzer, *Structural Hearing* (New York: Dover Publications, 1952).
84. William Mitchell, *Elementary Harmony*, p. 3.
85. Ibid., p. 61.
86. Ibid., p. 62.
87. Rameau, *Traité de l'harmonie*, 2: 50.
88. Mitchell, pp. 38–39.
89. Ibid., p. 6.
90. Ibid.
91. Ibid., pp. 109–11.
92. Ibid.
93. Ibid., p. 152.
94. Ibid.
95. Ibid., p. 206.
96. Sessions, p. 248.
97. Allen Forte, *Tonal Harmony in Concept and Practice*, p. 3.
98. Ibid., p. 7.
99. Ibid., p. 42.
100. Ibid., p. 45.
101. Ibid., p. 74.
102. Ibid., p. 136.
103. Ibid., p. 174.
104. Ibid., p. 310.
105. Ibid., p. 340.
106. Ibid., p. 341.
107. Ibid., pp. 87–88.
108. Ibid., p. 88.

109. Ibid., p. 90.
110. Ibid., p. 91.
111. Ibid., p. 99.
112. Ibid., p. 107.
113. Ibid., p. 113.
114. Ibid., p. 100.

Chapter 5

1. Paul Harder, *Harmonic Materials in Tonal Music* (Boston: Allyn and Bacon, 1968), Preface, p. v.
2. Richard Goldman, *Harmony in Western Music*, p. 69.
3. A good study of the wide diversity of analytical symbols is George T. Jones's *Symbols Used in Music Analysis*. Jones surveys the analytical symbols used in a large number of harmony texts in the United States and makes recommendations for a standard system. He also surveys chord symbols used in popular sheet-music.
4. Wallace Berry, *Form in Music*, p. 10n.
5. Goldman, Preface, p. ix.

Selected Bibliography

Treatises and Texts

Alchin, Carolyn. *Applied Harmony*. 2 vols. Revised by Vincent Jones. Los Angeles: L. R. Jones, 1931.

Berry, Wallace. *Form in Music*. Englewood Cliffs, N. J.: Prentice-Hall, 1966.

Bullis, Carleton. *Harmonic Forms*. Cleveland: Clifton Press, 1933.

Chadwick, George. *Harmony*. Boston: B. F. Wood, 1897.

Christ, William; DeLone, R.; Kliewer, V.; Rowell, L.; and Thompson, W. *Materials and Structure of Music*. 2 vols. Englewood Cliffs, N. J.: Prentice-Hall, 1966.

Cutter, Benjamin. *Harmonic Analysis*. Boston: O. Ditson, 1902.

Day, Alfred. *A Treatise on Harmony*. London: Cramer, Beale & Co., 1845.

Faisst, Immanuel Gottlob. *Harmonielehre nach Immanuel Faisst*. Adapted by Heinrich Lang. Stuttgart: Sulze & Galler, n.d.

Foote, Arthur. *Modulation and Related Harmonic Questions*. Boston: A. P. Schmidt, 1919.

Foote, Arthur, and Spalding, Walter. *Modern Harmony in its Theory and Practice*. Boston: A. P. Schmidt, 1905.

Forte, Allen. *Tonal Harmony in Concept and Practice*. New York: Holt, Rinehart, & Winston, 1962.

Goetschius, Percy. *The Material Used in Musical Composition*. New York: G. Schirmer, 1889.

———. *The Structure of Music*. Philadelphia: T. Presser, 1934.

———. *The Theory and Practice of Tone-Relations*. New York: G. Schirmer, 1892.

Goldman, Richard Franko. *Harmony in Western Music*. New York: W. W. Norton, 1965.

Heacox, Arthur E. *Harmony for Ear, Eye, and Keyboard*. Boston: O. Ditson, 1922.

Hindemith, Paul. *Traditional Harmony*. 2 vols. London: Schott & Co., 1943.
Jadassohn, Solomon. *Manual of Harmony*. Translated by Paul Torek and H.
     B. Pasmore. Leipzig: Breitkopf & Hartel, 1884.
Leighton, George. *Harmony, Analytical and Applied*. Boston: B. F. Wood,
     1927.
Macfarren, George. *Six Lectures on Harmony*. 3rd ed. London: Longmans,
     Green & Co., 1882.
McHose, Allen Irvine. *Basic Principles of the Technique of 18th and 19th Century
     Composition*. New York: Appleton-Century-Crofts, 1951.
————. *The Contrapuntal Harmonic Technique of the 18th Century*. New York:
     Appleton-Century-Crofts, 1947.
Mitchell, William J. *Elementary Harmony*. New York: Prentice-Hall, 1939.
Ottman, Robert. *Advanced Harmony*. Englewood Cliffs, N. J.: Prentice-
     Hall, 1961.
————. *Elementary Harmony*. Englewood Cliffs, N. J.: Prentice-Hall, 1961.
Ouseley, Rev. Sir Frederick A. Gore. *A Treatise on Harmony*. Oxford:
     Clarendon Press, 1868.
Parker, James C. D. *Manual of Harmony and Thorough Bass*. Boston: Nathan
     Richardson, 1855.
Parkhurst, Howard Elmore. *Harmony*. New York: C. Fischer, 1908.
Piston, Walter. *Harmony*. New York: W. W. Norton, 1941.
————. *Principles of Harmonic Analysis*. Boston: E. C. Schirmer, 1938.
Prout, Ebenezer. *Harmony, its Theory and Practice*. London: Augener & Co.,
     1889.
Rameau, Jean-Philippe. *Traité de l'harmonie*. Paris: Jean Baptiste
     Christophe Ballard, 1722. Facsimile. New York: Broude Bros., 1965.
Richter, Ernst Freidrich. *Manual of Harmony*. Translated by John P.
     Morgan. New York: G. Schirmer, 1867.
Robinson, Franklin. *Aural Harmony*. 2nd ed. 2 vols. New York: Coleman-
     Hill, 1936.
Schenker, Heinrich. *Der Freie Satz*. Vienna: Universal Ed., 1935.
————. *Harmony*. Ed. Oswald Jones. Translated by Elizabeth Mann
     Borgese. Chicago: University of Chicago Press, 1954.
Sessions, Roger. *Harmonic Practice*. New York: Harcourt, Brace & Co.,
     1951.
Shepard, Frank. *Harmony Simplified*. New York: G. Schirmer, 1896.
Shir-Clif, Justine; Jay, Stephen; and Rauscher, Donald J. *Chromatic
     Harmony*. New York: Free Press, 1965.
Tapper, Thomas. *First Year Harmony*. Boston: O. Ditson, 1908.
Tweedy, Donald. *Manual of Harmonic Technic*. Boston: O. Ditson, 1928.
Weber, Gottfried. *Theory of Musical Composition*. Translated by James F.
     Warner. Boston: O. Ditson, 1846.
Wedge, George. *Advanced Ear Training and Sight-Singing*. New York: G.
     Schirmer, 1922.

————. *Applied Harmony*. 2 vols. New York: G. Schirmer, 1930–31.
Wood, Carl Paige. *The Texture of Music*. Boston: Bruce Humphries, 1931.
York, Francis. *Harmony Simplified*. Boston: O. Ditson, 1897.

Other Sources

Carroll, Mother Catherine Agnes. "Percy Goetschius, an American Theorist and Teacher." Ph.D. dissertation, University of Rochester, 1957.
Dwight, John S. "Reviews," in *Dwight's Journal of Music*. May 1, 1852, p. 29; July 25, 1874, p. 270; December 22, 1855, p. 94.
Elson, Louis. *The History of American Music*. New York: Macmillan & Co., 1904.
Jones, George T. *Symbols Used in Music Analysis*. Washington: Catholic University of America, 1964.
Ortmann, Otto. "Notes on the Nature of Harmony." *Musical Quarterly* 6 (July, 1921): 367–75.
Riemann, Hugo. *History of Music Theory*. Vol. 3. Translated by William Mickelson. Lincoln: University of Nebraska Press, 1977.
————. "Faisst, Immanuel," and "Richter, E. F. E.," in *Musik Lexikon*, 12th ed. Mainz: B. Schotts Sohne, 1959.
Shepherd, Arthur. " 'Papa' Goetschius in Retrospect." *Musical Quarterly* 29 (July, 1944): 307–18.
Shirlaw, Matthew. *The Theory and Nature of Harmony*. Sarasota, Fla.: Birchard Coar, 1970.

Index

Pythagorean system, in Goetschius, 41–43; in Tweedy, 100; in Wedge, 110

Rameau, Jean-Philippe, 5, 9, 12, 54, 167; in McHose, 153–56, 160
Rauscher, Donald J., 150
Rhythm, harmonic, in Piston, 141–44; in Sessions, 150–51; in Christ, et al., 151
Richter, Ernst F., 3–4, 16–19, 74, 163, 185–86; influence on American writers, 74–78, 88, 185
Robinson, Franklin, 90–97, 99, 104–5, 107, 108, 182–83
Roman numeral symbols. *See* Symbols, analytical
Rowell, Lewis, 147, 151

Salzer, Felix, 165
Schenker, Heinrich, 162–65; influence on American writers, 165–80
Schneider, Friedrich, 16
Second inversion, triads in, in Richter, 19; in Faisst, 21; in Goetschius, 50; in Shepard, 78; in Piston, 134; in Mitchell, 169; in Forte, 176
Secondary dominant, 14, 164; in Piston, 127–28, 138–39, 148; in Hindemith, 146; in Sessions, 146–47; in Christ, et al., 147; in Berry, 148. *See also* Apparent dominants, "Attendant" chord, Embellishing chords, Parenthesis chords
Secondary triads, in Faisst, 20–21; in Goetschius, 46–47; in Shepard, 77; in Chadwick, 77; in Foote and Spalding, 77, 81
Sessions, Roger, 146–47, 148, 149–51, 172
Seventh, chords of the, in Weber, 10, 13; in Richter, 17–18; in Faisst, 21–22; in Goetschius, 50–52; in Shepard, 77; in Parkhurst, 77; in Cutter, 85–86; in Wedge, 112; in Piston, 137–38; in McHose, 149; in Sessions, 149; in Mitchell, 169; in Forte, 175

Shepard, Frank, 75–78, 116–18
Shir-Clif, Justine, 150
Shirlaw, Matthew, 25
Six Lectures on Harmony (Macfarren), 4, 26
Sorge, Georg Andress, 6
Spalding, Walter, 74–75, 79–81, 114
Stainer, Sir John, 4
Statistical basis, 153–57
Structure of Music (Goetschius), 114–5
Subdominant, derivation of, in Victorian theory, 27; in Goetschius, 43–44, 51–52, 54; in Robinson, 94; in Ortmann, 98–99; in Tweedy, 101, 103–4; conclusion, 183–84
Subordinate triads. *See* Secondary triads
Symbols, analytical, Weber's, 14–16; Richter's, 18; Faisst's, 22; Goetschius's, 50, 56–57; Chadwick's, 75–76; York's, 76; Cutter's, 76; Tweedy's, 104–5; Wedge's, 112; McHose's, 159, 185; conclusion, 185

Tapper, Thomas, 75, 77
Texture of Music (Wood), 114
Theory and Practice of Musical Composition (Marx), 2–3
Theory and Practice of Tone Relations (Goetschius), 38–39, 65, 74
Theory of Musical Composition (Weber), 1–2, 4–5
Thompson, William, 147, 151
Tonal Harmony in Concept and Practice (Forte), 172
"Tone-relations," 40–45
Tonicization, in Schenker, 164; in Sessions, 172
Tonwille, der (Schenker), 164
Traite de l'harmonie (Rameau), 54, 167
Transient modulations, in Weber, 14; in Goetschius, 59–61; American theorists' rejection of, 115–28; in York, 115–16; in Foote, 121; in Tweedy, 121–22
Treatise on Harmony (Day), 23–24, 27
Treatise on Harmony (Ouseley), 24–25, 27